this is
OUR
TIME
Jim Ritchie

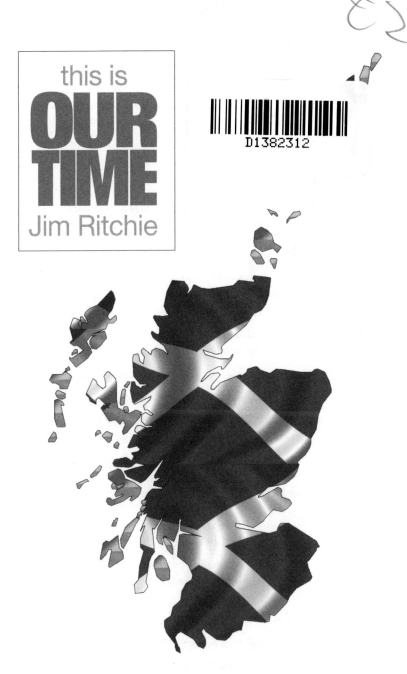

THE DAWN OF A NEW DAY FOR THE CHURCH IN SCOTLAND

Published for Jim Ritchie and The Scotland Trust by Verité CM Limited
8 St John's Parade, Alinora Crescent, Goring by Sea
West Sussex BN12 4HJ
United Kingdom
+44 (0) 1903 241975

email: enquiries@veritecm.com
Web: www.veritecm.com

British Library Cataloguing Data
A catalogue record of this book is available from The British Library

Typesetting by Verité CM Ltd

Printed in England

DEDICATION

This book is dedicated to the glory of God, for the people of Scotland and to the memory of my parents Jim and Mary Ritchie, 'Together forever, in Immanuel's land'

CONTENTS

ACKNOWLEDGEMENTS

I would like to thank the following people for their encouragement and support over 25 years of ministry and as I have embarked upon writing this book.

- To my incredible wife Maggie. You mean more to me than words can say and as you know I say a lot of words! My wife, lover, best friend, prayer warrior and constant companion.

- To my amazing children; Pam, Dawn, Andy, Becky and Gavin. You inspire me and never cease to amaze me in how you all go for God, follow your dreams with passion and commitment and forgive your dad when I embarrass you!

- To Sam Hocking- welcome to the family!

- To our families. Thanks for years of love and support. There are a lot of you so I will just mention you by family names! We love and pray for you all: The Ritchies, The Rowans, The Taylors, The Hendrys, The Cruickshanks and The Grants.

- To all of The Scotland Trust. We share a dream and a passion for God and our nation. Thank you so much for your continual encouragement and inspiration; Tommy and Donna Macneil, Innes Macleod, Gordon Cowan, Kenny Borthwick, Andrea Wigglesworth, Brian Taylor and of course Maggie Ritchie. Also thanks to Maria, Ann, Morag, Peter, Jenny and all their families for letting them spend some of their precious time on this ministry.

- To John Swinton for your friendship over many years. You always help me to see the Kingdom in wonderful new ways. Thanks for help in editing and shaping this book and for writing the foreword. Thanks to Alison and the kids for allowing him to spend more time in his study because of me!

- To Liz Goodge for proof reading and correcting my grammar! Also to Liz and husband Andrew for your unbelievable love and support as we have walked this new path. Not to mention introducing us to Hotel Chocolat and Hillbrae beef!

- To all the Triumph team over the years as we rocked all over the world! Gordon and Ann, Andi and Hillary, Stevie, Heather, Campbell and Sandra, George, Alan and Melv; and all our kids, The Triumph Babies, who went to so many of our gigs and had their hearing damaged!

- To Bill and Sylvia Smith for your friendship and always understanding and trusting us and God. Thanks for that day at Cupar and for years of good accounting!

- To my many friends and colleagues in Oldmachar Church in our eight year adventure there. Much of this book is 'our' story. There are too many of you to name personally and some of you get a name check in the book anyway! Please know I love you all. No other church would have welcomed us back and then sent us out again with such love, faith and understanding.

- The Council of Reference for The Scotland Trust as you support us and stand with us in this calling to our land. Especially Peter Neilson and Fred Drummond for their kind words on the book

- To Paul Burley for an inspirational logo.

- To Point 1 in Stornoway for superb graphic and printing; especially Innes, Caskie and Philip.

- Chris Powell and all at Verite for making this process so simple and for an amazingly professional job. Also to Nancy and Ray Goudie for pointing me to Verite and for friendship and inspiration.

- All my football and band buddies. You know who you are!

FOREWORD

"The man who saw it has given testimony, and his testimony is true. He knows that he tells the truth, and he testifies so that you also may believe."

JOHN 19:35

It's interesting in reading John's gospel just how many times the word 'testimony' appears. John is constantly telling us that testifying – speaking out the story of what God has done in our lives – is a primary mode of evangelism. As we tell our story of what the Lord has done for us, others are enabled to receive the gift and the opportunity to grasp what God has done for them. When the story is heard, understood and accepted, salvation begins. Indeed if Jim Ritchie is correct in the things he offers to us in this book, we might even understand conversion as *that point in our lives when our story becomes His-story.*

This book contains Jim's story... and more. The book testifies to what God has done and is doing in his life. It is a place where his testimony becomes public. As we are guided through his story we are drawn into the presence of God as God has revealed God's self in the life of a disciple and, perhaps, a prophet. I use the term 'prophet' here in a quite particular way. Prophecy is not simply the act of foretelling the future. Prophecy has to do with bringing to mind the active presence of God in the past, in the present and in the future. This is precisely the prophetic task that Jim Ritchie brings to our notice in this book. In a time when the churches in Scotland are showing depressing decline, Jim's story reminds us of the promises of God in the past, the ways in which these promises sustain us in the present and how they point us towards new and exciting futures.

He offers this book to us as *a gift of assurance*; a testimony that affirms the promise that Jesus is precisely whom we believe Him to be and that despite circumstances, God *is in control!* In testifying to the transforming power of God as it has been revealed in his life, Jim helps us to share in a vibrant memory of hope. This memory can not only sustain us in our present trials but, if we remember correctly, can drive us out in the power of the Holy Spirit to make history. The message of this book is that history should not be viewed as something that has simply gone before us; rather, *history is something that is being made in the present.*

The past – where we have been – is vitally important; but the future is where the promise is fulfilled. *God is inviting us to participate in the making of history.*

> *Jesus is precisely whom we believe Him to be and that despite circumstances, God is in control!*

In telling his story, Jim offers a prophetic voice that helps us to remember the promise of God: "Never will I leave you; never will I forsake you." (Hebrews 13:5) By inviting people to listen to his testimony and to allow that story to bolster their faith, Jim aims to ensure that the church has the resources not only to stand firm in the midst of its current trials, but also to grow, or perhaps better, be resurrected into precisely the shape and form that God requires for the challenges of today.

At one level we might despair that the Scottish churches are declining and dying. But at another level we should be inspired: death and resurrection are the pattern of the gospel. From the death of the church will emerge new life, new possibilities, new stories, new hope. The Spirit is moving! Jim Ritchie calls us to listen and to allow our stories to be transformed by our new calling: *to become the makers of history in our time!*

If that doesn't excite us then we have clearly been listening to the wrong stories! I commend this book to its readers. It is my hope and my prayer that in accepting the gift that Jim Ritchie offers to us in this book, together we can discover a new depth to our own stories and perhaps more importantly, begin to recognise the ways in which our stories are deeply interconnected with one another and with the story of God. In a world that is rapidly fragmenting, losing hope and losing sight of God, there may not be a greater gift.

John Swinton
Professor in Practical Theology and Pastoral Care
University of Aberdeen

INTRODUCTION

There are so many good Christian books published today and so many interesting new titles coming onto the shelves of our Christian bookstores all of the time that it is difficult to know what to buy. So whenever I pick up a book in a bookshop the first thing I do now is to look closely at the introduction and contents to decide whether I will buy it or not. As I am spoilt for choice something has to take me beyond a cursory glance and make me decide that this is worth paying money for! When I look at a book I want to know what it is about, who is writing it, what their story is, what they have got to say and most importantly, why this book should matter to me! If it does not grab me in any of those categories right away I will probably put the book down and look at something else.

Therefore, as you have a look at this book and make that same choice, I want to give you a little insight into me and my story and why I think you may want to part with some of your hard earned cash to buy it!

The first thing I want to say about me and this book is that neither is pretentious! Over the years people have often told me that I should write a book and share some of the things I have done and said in my ministry with others. My response to this at first was always, 'Me, write a book? That will never happen. Who would want to read what I have to say?' However, as time passed and as my ministry developed, I started to believe that all of us have something to say that is worth listening to... and that included me! Perhaps I did have some things I wanted to share? My problem then became not so much a lack of belief in my ability to write a book but working out how on earth I would find the time to write one amidst the unrelenting pressures of local parish ministry.

As you are holding my book in your hand now it is self-evident that I found both the confidence and the time to write it and I hope it will be inspiring and challenging to all who decide to buy it and read it! This book comes at a new juncture in my life as I move from local church ministry to a national role within a new ministry in our land, The Scotland Trust, which provided me with both the time and the reason to write this book. At the heart of The Scotland Trust is a desire to see revival in our nation and renewal in our church and a core belief that not only can we hope to see this happen but we can dare to believe that it is imminent and that we are the generation who are going to see it and live in it.

'*This is our time*' is both my personal story of 25 years in ministry and my vision for the future for the church in Scotland and beyond. The book is divided into three main parts. Firstly I begin by telling my story and what has shaped me as a person and in my ministry. This is a very personal reflection and I have called it '*Finding my place in His-story*'. I hope that as you read my story it will help you reflect on yours and see where God has been clearly working in your life and shaping who you are.

Then I move on to draw out some lessons and principles that have emerged from my ministry. This second section focuses on new models of ministry derived from my experience and calling. This section is titled: '*Making History Today*'. The point here is to use what God has done in my life and ministry to point towards new ways of being church which may be applicable to other churches in Scotland and beyond.

Finally, I close the book by looking at what kind of people make significant Kingdom differences in their life, church and community in the last section called, '*Choosing to be a History Maker*'. This is where I want to encourage each reader that it is not just some 'special' people who make big differences for God, rather, it is ordinary people like you and me who, when we make the right kind of choices, change our destiny and the world around us. I have always believed that we can either make history or watch it being made. My cry to each reader is – *choose to make history*!

Overarching all of this is a heart for the people and church in my nation of Scotland and my deep conviction that 'this is our time'. Our time to be all we can be for God, our time to see Him move in a new way in our nation and our time to do the things we need to do to see His Kingdom come and His will done on earth as it is in heaven! However, although the book is written by a Scotsman principally for Scotland in this time, you don't you have to be Scottish or ministering and working in Scotland for this book to speak to you and your situation. I believe all the principles I apply in the book are Biblical and transferrable to the culture and context in which any reader is working.

My own story unfolds and is woven into the very essence and texture of this book. Yet, before I take you on our journey together it might be helpful for me to introduce myself. If I offer you a bit of my history it will be easier for you to see my place and indeed our place in His-story.

I was born and brought up in a small village called Caldercruix on the outskirts of Airdrie in Lanarkshire, Scotland. As a sixteen year old I gave my life to Jesus through the ministry of my local Church of Scotland minister Rev. Jim Martin and the witness of my family, as I saw for the first time the vibrant reality of faith in Christ. I later grew in my faith and understanding of God's Word and the power of His Spirit in my life under the next two Ministers of Caldercruix Church; Rev. Bob Nelson and Rev. Charles Finnie.

Since giving my life to Jesus my passion and purpose for living has been singular; to know Him more and to share the amazing relationship I have found in Him with others. From the earliest days of my faith I have had a huge heart for evangelism, worship and communication; making the message of Jesus as relevant and interesting as possible, particularly to the younger generation. Within weeks of becoming a Christian I was speaking and singing at youth fellowships, churches and open air services in my village and in Airdrie, then further afield with my church youth group and in Church of Scotland summer missions. This was very fertile soil in which to grow in my faith and, as my faith grew, so did the desire that was stirring within me to give my life to God in full-time ministry.

Up to that point my dream-life scenario, like many young boys, was either a professional football player or a rock star! I was a decent football player and played at a good standard at school and boys club level which led to trials and offers of trials with some professional teams in Scotland and England. I played with some tremendous players in those days who went on to become household names at the very top of the game but I never quite made it to that level. However, God had another plan for my life that was not in scoring goals but winning souls! Much as I continued to love football I knew that my own path was to be different and my passion to work for God grew to the point where I could not ignore it any longer.

So after a summer mission in Peebles in 1982, where I met the love of my life, Maggie, we both went to Bible College to begin our preparation for a life in full-time ministry. My rock star dream was less based in reality during my teenage years than my football dream was and at that time my hopes of rock stardom were honed in the humble surroundings of my bedroom, in front of a mirror with a hair brush for a microphone and a tennis racket for a guitar, singing along to Rod Stewart, Queen and Deep Purple. Yet in my early twenties after completing my Bible College diploma I did manage to get my hands on a real microphone and guitar as I formed a Christian rock band, 'Triumph', with friends Gordon Cowan, Steve Nelson and Andi Tooth.

However, Triumph was not about being a rock star it was an attempt to communicate a contemporary expression of the Gospel through rock music to young people, who at that time had little other than traditional church to relate life and faith in Jesus to. Over the next ten years Triumph recorded four albums, played over 700 live concerts all over the UK and Europe to an estimated combined live audience of over 500,000 people[i]. I know this is not on the same level as U2 or The Rolling Stones, but for a young Scottish Christian band at that time it was beyond our wildest dreams. Triumph had the privilege of sharing our faith in Jesus with so many young people who otherwise would not have heard of His love for them in this way. Without doubt the most joyful legacy I have from those days is in meeting people who are now in church ministry or leadership who tell me they came to faith in Jesus at a Triumph gig! It was also a time when Christian music was starting to become more professional and accepted in the church and amongst secular media, so along with contemporaries such as Martyn Joseph, Split Level and Heartbeat we built on the work of the early pioneers of British Gospel music like John Pantry, Adrian Snell, Garth Hewitt and The Barrett Band to help pave the way for what came next in British contemporary Christian music and the explosion in worship.

In 1992 Triumph came to an end and at that time I felt a clear, yet slightly surprising, call to ministry within the Church of Scotland. I had a lot of respect for many of the ministers I knew, but I also had a stereotype of what one was like and I was not it! However, I tested and trusted the call I was feeling and applied to the Church to attend a selection school to see if this sense of calling was reciprocated. I was accepted by the church as a candidate for ministry and was required to complete five years of theological study at New College in Edinburgh, as well as a number of practical placements in local churches. This was all a huge shift from what I had been doing in the band and a massive cultural shock to me at first. However, I knew it was a means to an end and I was doing what God wanted me to. I was licensed to minister within the Church of Scotland in my home parish of Caldercruix in October 1997 and this was a great night for my family and I as well as the

---

i   For those who never got to see Triumph live or for those wanting to re-live some memories, visit 'Youtube' and search under 'Triumph UK – Hope for my children'

congregation who had never had a 'local lad' licensed to ministry in its long history. After my licensing I spent fourteen months on probation as an assistant to Rev. Alex Millar at New Scone and St. Martins in Perth which was a great experience where I learnt a lot and ministered amongst some wonderful people.

On completing my probationary period the next 10 years of my life and ministry were spent in Canada and at Oldmachar Church in Bridge of Don in Aberdeen. The first few chapters of the book tell some of that story in relation to our family's moves back and forth from Scotland to Canada and much of what I write throughout comes from the lessons I learnt in leading the church at Oldmachar.

Nonetheless, it is important to say at this juncture that I am convinced that the Oldmachar story is a very important one for the church in Scotland and for all who are working to build a faith community in their own place today as it is a significant story of a 'success' in contextual, contemporary ministry[ii]. Yet I have to state that Oldmachar did not work because I was particularly clever or because the congregation or local area was just right for such a success. It worked and continues to do so, because the Biblical principles for growing and building a body of God's people in a particular time and place have always been prized above all traditions and personal agendas. Although it is far from perfect the results have been significant and I believe are worth considering.

The most recent part of my story is the one I am living now in this new calling as National Director of The Scotland Trust. This calling comes from a conviction of what God is doing in Scotland and what I believe is coming next as the church that He is birthing in these days emerges. I believe that what comes next is my story, your story; our story! So if you are still with me at this point please read on and be encouraged that what you and I do next with our lives is of historical significance for our generation and our nation, because 'This is our time'.

---

ii   For a look at what Oldmachar is about go to Youtube and search under Oldmachar Church

CHAPTER 1: OUR TIME

"There is a time for everything, and a season for every activity under heaven"

KING SOLOMON, IN ECCLESIASTES 3:1 NIV

Solomon was an interesting character. He was the third King of Israel and heir to the throne chosen by the great King David and, apart from Joshua who followed Moses, perhaps no-one else in the history of God's people ever had a harder act to follow. Nonetheless, Solomon was the man who first built God's temple in Jerusalem. He was the author of Ecclesiastes and Song of Songs as well as most of the Proverbs and a few Psalms.

In his time he was known as a king, a trader, a diplomat, a patron of the arts, and a collector of many items of great worth and beauty, including wives! Yes, he was a passionate man in every sense of the word. In history his name is synonymous with wisdom and antiquity tells us that, after he sought this above all things from God, he was the wisest man who had ever lived[iii]. However, for such a wise man he did make some real clangers of mistakes and serious errors of judgement, so there's hope for us all! Like many a powerful man throughout history, his main weaknesses became apparent when his decision-making was compromised by his need to fulfil his personal desires. This often involved women. Yet overall his reign as king of Israel was a great success and he did things that even David did not do. Primarily, of course, Solomon built the temple.

---

iii See 1 Kings 3

Following on from David's reign, Solomon's could have been a damp squib. He could have lived and died in David's huge royal shadow, and he could have been nobody in Israel's history. Even worse, when asked by God what he desired most, he could have asked for nothing more than riches and honour and so ended up in the 'Bad Kings' hall of shame that runs through the Old Testament. But he didn't and part of the reason for this was that he knew that this was his time, and this was *his* moment and he wasn't about to let it pass him by. He wasn't David, and never would be, so there was no point in trying to copy or repeat his reign. He would be God's man in *his* time. The words he writes in Ecclesiastes chapter 3, probably near the end of his time as king, are the words of a man who knew that his time was limited, his day would come and go and the only things that mattered were those that would last after he was gone; the legacy he would leave at the end of his God-given time on earth.

I'd like to think that when Solomon was given his Godly-wisdom at the start of his kingship this truth penetrated his heart so deeply that he lived his life with all the passion and fervour he could, that he made whatever difference he could and, above all, that he then lived and died for nothing but the glory and honour of God. Is there any better way to live?

> *History makers, like Solomon, are those who do things no-one else has ever done, who make a mark on their generation that is both deep and lasting.*

History makers, like Solomon, are those who do things no-one else has ever done, who make a mark on their generation that is both deep and lasting. But above all history-makers are generally people of their time, who know this is *their* day, *their* moment, and *their* chance to make a difference. They are the people who will not stop until the light goes on; who will run harder to the line; who will campaign more to abolish social evil; who will give their life for their cause; who will take their stand for Jesus and not back off, because they can do nothing else. It's how they were made. Everything they have chosen to be and all that they are would mean nothing if they did any less.

What I find incredible though, is that most history makers I have ever read about and the few that I have met, appear to be by and large just ordinary people who did extra-ordinary things in their time. They are people who were not perfect, who made mistakes and often got things wrong. They didn't necessarily seek the limelight, but were simply aware of their destiny – the reason they were put on this earth – and so pursued it in a way that perhaps others didn't. Those Kingdom history makers whose names are written large over God's story in the Bible and throughout church history have mostly just been ordinary women and men who, empowered by an extra-ordinary God, did things that literally changed the world. I have always been fascinated by such people, whether in biblical history or in the secular world history we were taught at school and what made them make the difference they did.

In particular when I was growing up I was consumed by Scottish history and those who made it. Dad had great books about Robert the Bruce and William Wallace which I loved to read, long before 'Braveheart' made them fashionable and he also had some really interesting stories about The Covenanters; martyrs like Peden and Wishart whose evangelistic zeal, prophetic edge and heart for God and His Word were both inspirational and humbling. I can remember reading these stories and wanting to be like these men who made such an impact on their nation in their day, just as much as I dreamed of being the next footballing legend like Denis Law or Billy Bremner or Kenny Dalglish.

We all have within us the potential for greatness, but only some grasp it and go for it. I have always believed that we can either make history or watch it being made; we can either write it or read about it. History makers are in a nation's heart and courage is in its very soil, it just needs to be unearthed in individuals who know their place in their time. Scotland is a nation with a rich and interesting history, and for such a relatively small country the Scots have played a large role in the world's development; socially, in medicine, science and in the world of business and finance.

The church in Scotland also has an equally strong history and has a world-wide missionary legacy which very few other nations have. In the years I was a parish minister in Aberdeen I met many believers from overseas, particularly from Africa, who could trace back the coming of The Gospel to their land, their village and ultimately to their own life, to a Scot who was sent out by the Scottish church in the name of Jesus. There are some like Mary Slessor and David Livingstone whose names and heroic acts are forever linked to the missionary endeavours of the Scottish church. There are also others, ordinary heroes, history-makers whose names would be recognised by very few people. But God knew them and used them powerfully.

In Scotland there is also a rich heritage of God moving in the nation in astounding ways from the Reformation in John Knox's day and the spiritual and social transformation of our cities through people like Thomas Chalmers, to great revivals within communities around the country in places as diverse as Cambuslang and the Isle of Lewis. Events which without exaggeration could be said helped shape and define individual communities and the state of the nation just as much as Solomon's temple did in Jerusalem.

Whenever I fly back to Scotland from holidays or trips abroad and walk through the arrivals lounge at Glasgow, Edinburgh or Aberdeen airports I always smile when I see the billboards on the walls greeting all travellers which say, *'Scotland, the best small country in the world'*. This says everything about us Scots! A wee bit of *'Here's tae us wha's like us?'* [iv] and a wee bit of 'proud humility' (yes I know it's an oxy-moron) on the world stage, that we know we're small in comparison to others, but great nonetheless. I like that

---

iv   A colloquial Scots' phrase meaning, 'here's to us, who is like us?'

about our nation and it displays something of the growing self-belief and self-confidence which is returning to Scotland after years of self-doubt, gloom and small-mindedness which seemed to pervade the land and its media for a while.

Scots seem to be starting to believe in themselves again and are once more making a mark on the world stage. We're even starting to win the occasional football match! So what about the church in Scotland? Well, the truth is that on the surface the church in Scotland would appear to be at the completely opposite end of the scale to this. It appears to be a church that is in terminal decline, with falling numbers, ageing congregations, little money, fewer prospective full-time leaders and little reason for confidence that anything is going to turn this around. Most worryingly of all, within the church there seems to be an apparent inability to adapt to the changes in our nation's culture and be a relevant voice and transformative force in today's society.

> *Within the church there seems to be an apparent inability to adapt to the changes in our nation's culture and be a relevant voice and transformative force in today's society.*

The days of Knox, Peden, Chalmers, and Slessor and the revivals seem a very long way away to many. In some places these ghosts of revivals past and the church as it once was seem to haunt and taunt the contemporary church about its failure. However, as with many things, particularly the things in which God is involved, first appearances are not necessarily the way things really are.

Sure, the traditional, mainstream church no longer has the place of influence it once had in our land or around the world and the numbers of people going to organised Sunday church services overall has indeed dropped significantly. Nevertheless there's something else happening and it is inherently connected to the very heart of God, who is the God of resurrection and life and the God of times and seasons. For as an old church is dying, a new one is being birthed! I am convinced that this is the time for a new church, and a new move of God's people in this land to emerge.

It will not be like what went before and neither should it be, for that was then and this is now and God gives each generation the responsibility for reaching their communities in their time. What may have worked in the past will not necessarily work today or tomorrow and a new wineskin is required. As I look around the country I see this beginning to happen. As I see what God is doing through ordinary people with a passion for Him, my heart is stirred. I see a new generation rising up within the church who are committed and courageous, who are not sentimental about what once was and are not held back by what might have been. They are just passionate about Jesus, desperate to reach out to their generation and aware that this is their moment, their time to do it.

The history makers of this day are beginning to appear and there are many of them. They will write the story of what the church will become in this land in the days ahead. They are normal people who will take their chance, pay the price and go after their destiny in their time. Maybe you will be one of them? I know I long to be. For like many Christians in this land I am no longer content just to read with joy of how God is moving in other places around the world today, or yearn for how He once moved here. I want to see Him move here again.

I believe that this is right at the heart of God's timing for our land. For in increasing measure the prophetic voice has told us that God is going to do a new thing in Scotland and the frequency and urgency of that voice tells us that the time is closer than ever.

I know I am not alone in believing that a new day is coming for the church in Scotland. Indeed it is already here and so we must pray, plan and prepare and work with expectancy of this new day unfolding. The premise is simple; if we believe that our nation desperately needs to hear the Good News and see the Kingdom demonstration of God's love in a relevant, significant and effective way today, then we have to believe that we are the ones who can do that, and now is the time!

Our nation will only listen and ultimately will only be transformed when the church moves from a place of irrelevance and insignificance to having a relevant voice and a crucial influence on the nation at every level. That means from the kids on our streets to the heads of government and political figures; from within families to the business community; through education, social care and training establishments; and in the worlds of sport, art, music and entertainment. In other words in every level of society as we know it.

None of this will happen within the walls of the church alone and it will not happen by just doing the things we have done before, hoping that they will now start to work. A businessman who is one of my closest friends once said to me that the church is often guilty of one of the first signs of madness; to keep doing the same things and yet expect different results. If we want to see things we have never seen before we have to do things we have never done before! If established churches are to survive they need fresh encouragement and fresh resourcing to reach out effectively to those around them and be an authentic contemporary expression of Christian community today and tomorrow. Equally, new churches must be planted and new leaders raised up, equipped, mentored and released to find new ways of being the church for a new generation.

Scripture and history teach us that whenever God moves in a new way He always gives that generation the calling and blueprint for the shape and values of the new church and missional approach that is needed for that time, if they will listen and courageously obey the Spirit's voice and leading. So whatever the new church that emerges in Scotland is to look like, I am convinced that it is God's desire that it is marked with a particular urgency to win the lost, heal the broken, love and care for the poor and despised, and create a new tomorrow for the young people of Scotland. For if we don't who else will?

As a church we have to recognise the great gift to Scotland of many people from the body of Christ around the world coming here to bless the church and reach our nation and it is really encouraging when I meet people from around the world whom God has called here as missionaries. God knows we need them. But the church in Scotland, with a heart for Scotland must also now take the initiative, believe in who they are in Christ and bear the responsibility to reach their own nation, change the church and pay the price required to see it happen. We have to go out as missionaries in our own midst. Then perhaps in the days to come, Scotland may once again be known throughout the world as a sending nation, with a missionary heart that beats with all the urgency of heaven.

We are not responsible for what happened in previous generations and it was not our call to reach them or the world in which they lived. Only history can now declare how they did. But we are responsible for how we reach out in Jesus' name to the nation, cities, towns and villages in which God has placed us, today and tomorrow. What will history write about our efforts? There is a huge job to be done and many people working together, committed to the cause of the King and His Kingdom will be needed to see a new day come. However, God is with us and 'The earth is the Lord's and everything in it', [v] so we should be convinced that He will provide all we need to do the job. After all, Scotland is part of Jesus' inheritance and He will work with us to win it for Him.

In 'Scots Wha Hae' [vi] Robert Burns writes, 'now's the day and now's the hour'. From a Kingdom perspective I believe this to be true. As King Solomon came to recognise, there is indeed 'a time for everything'. As the church in this land can we dare to believe that? That this is Scotland's time?

---

v   See Psalm 33:5

vi   'Scots wha hae' written by Robert Burns

CHAPTER 2: SON OF SCOTLAND

"I see God giving you a new name.
He is writing it on your forehead, he is calling you 'Son of Scotland' "

God often calls the most unexpected people to the most unexpected jobs at the most unexpected times.

I have heard this often throughout my Christian life and seen it happen to people I know, but on 13th July 2004 it was about to happen to me. God was about to place a burden on my soul and a passion on my heart for the people and nation of Scotland, the likes of which I had never known. I have always loved Scotland and have always been a proud Scot and as I said in the first chapter, since I was a boy, I have loved Scottish culture and history and dreamt of being like some of its heroes. My love of Scotland was never in any doubt. But in a tent in St. Andrews this was going to go to another level.

> God was about to place a burden on my soul and a passion on my heart for the people and nation of Scotland, the likes of which I had never known.

It was during an evening visit to Clan Gathering 2004 with 4,000 other people around me that God was about to totally rock my world and give me a calling to the nation and people of Scotland that was stronger than anything I had ever felt. What was so unexpected and unusual in this is that I had just moved to Canada! I had gone to minister as part of a team ministry in a growing city-centre church in the city of Brantford, Ontario. We had only emigrated in April of that year and we had moved the family, all 7 of us and all of our belongings to Canada. We were working in a new church, living in a brand new home, our five kids Pam, Dawn, Andy, Becky and Gavin were in new schools and I had in every way left Scotland and the church in Scotland to work in Canada.

When we sat on the plane from Glasgow to Toronto on 6th May 2004 I knew we would be back in Scotland and had no doubt I would minister there again someday, but I never thought for a moment we would be back so soon. Now we were back in Scotland just 2 months later, on a visit for family reasons, to see my mum who was in hospital.

Our family had spent a lot of time in that hospital, Monklands General Hospital in Airdrie, that year. It had without doubt been the most difficult year in my life. I had accepted a call to go to the church in Canada, after 4 years ministering happily at Oldmachar Church of Scotland, in Bridge of Don under New Charge Development. Over those 4 years we had seen the church grow in many ways and God was very gracious in the encouragement we had received in our ministry. Then we felt it was time to move on to a new call and a new adventure.

However, in my last year at Oldmachar my dad tragically died. Jim Ritchie was a huge man in every way and an enormous influence on my life, both my personal character and on my relationship with God as my Father. When I was studying theology, I had sometimes heard people share how the concept of God as Father was either alien to them and meant nothing, or actually had very negative connotations of abuse, neglect and lack of love. In my pastoral ministry I also encountered this on occasion and it is a real problem for some to overcome in their walk of faith.

Whilst I could truly sympathise with those whose earthly father had left them with this barrier to God's fatherly love and care, I could not have felt differently. Because of the loving example of my own dad, when I became a Christian as a 16 year old, being able to trust a heavenly Father was the easiest thing in the world for me. I will always be grateful to my dad for this, and every day I pray my own five children will see the same in me.

Dad had worked in hard manual labour all his life. He was 6'3" tall, built like the side of a house and extremely strong. Not someone you ever wanted a slap from! Yet he was the kindest, most generous gentle giant you could ever meet. He had a great strength of character, a deep faith and a wonderful singing voice! He died at just 69 years of age and the last 6 months of his life were hard to bear as this huge man disappeared before our eyes. He lost many things in those last months, but his faith in Jesus wasn't one of them. I'll never forget the last time he and I were together on our own as we talked, prayed and sang his favourite hymn, 'In Immanuel's land', in his hospital room. His once strong voice was painfully weak, but his faith was as strong as a rock.

After he died, taking the decision to continue with the move to Canada was a very difficult one, but we had prayed it through so many times and felt we had to go. My mum found it hard to let us go, having just lost her husband, but she knew and loved God and gave us her blessing to leave.

The first few weeks in Canada were hard for a number of reasons and the team we were to work with had some real initial teething problems. But we had been in ministry for over 20 years and initially felt that in time it would all work out. However, as the days passed it was clear that this was not proving to be the case and we were in what was beginning to look like a nightmare scenario, at the other end of the world, working in a new team which was starting to look completely un-workable. To make matters worse, when we were only in Canada for a couple of weeks we heard that mum had been taken into hospital, and speaking to my sisters Sandra and Brenda on the phone I sensed all was not well. We kept an eye on things for a few weeks until I knew I should go and see her.

With all the expense of the emigration of a family of seven to Canada, initially I thought I would go back myself, but my wife Maggie and I both felt we should all go as a family and let the kids see their granny. I now know this was the prompting of God and will always be thankful that we heeded the Spirit's voice and all went together, for the lovely visit we all had with mum in her hospital room the day we arrived would be the last time we'd all be together and a couple of days later she died in the same hospital that dad had died in a year earlier.

Dad's loss was incredibly hard for our whole family, but to lose both of our parents so soon after each other was huge double blow. Mum and dad complemented each other well. Dad was known as 'big Jim' to everyone who knew him, and mum was known as 'wee Mary'. At just over 5 feet she was indeed quite wee, but what she lacked in the height department she made up for in character and personality. Mary Ritchie, maiden name Rowan, was of Irish roots and she was feisty, funny and formidable at times. She was not to be messed with! She gave the best, or worst (depending on how you look at it) rows you can ever imagine. I know because I got a few of them. My sisters would of course contest this, as they claim she let me away with murder!

Yet she had the kindest, softest heart underneath and she never stopped giving. She would give her last penny away to help someone and quite often over the years she went without to make sure her family had all they needed. Like dad she worked hard all her life and enjoyed simple pleasures, with her family being her pride and joy. Mum also had a very deep faith and was a real woman of prayer. Losing dad had been

> *She could not understand why, but she trusted God and His will.*

devastating to her but on the day of his funeral in Caldercruix Parish Church, as we gathered as a family before the service she prayed the most beautiful prayer of faith and trust I have ever heard. She could not understand why, but she trusted God and His will. In hindsight it might be said that mum couldn't live without dad and maybe she died of a broken heart. I guess we will never know until we see them in glory, but what was comforting to me was to know that they were together again and that they were with Jesus.

It was the night before mum's funeral that Maggie and I were at Clan Gathering in St. Andrews. It was one of those God-incidences that we were there just at that time. Maggie's parents, Dr Bill and Elizabeth Taylor live in St. Andrews after retiring from General Practice in Airdrie. Their home has always been open to us and they have blessed and supported us so many times over the years. Their home was once again a sanctuary for us in a difficult time. Whilst home to see my mum, Maggie's parents were looking after us, especially the kids as we drove back and forth to Airdrie and had given us some space to do something together that night.

During the day as we walked along the west sands of St. Andrews we saw people we knew who told us that Clan was happening that week and I immediately felt we should go that evening. Maggie agreed and all day something grew in me that God had something to say to me at Clan. I said to Maggie, 'I think God has a word for us tonight'. On the way to the tent where the meeting was held I felt a strong sense of an imminent word from God growing and as we walked along the street I repeated to Maggie, 'I really think God has a word for us tonight'.

> I can't say that I particularly heard or felt anything from God as we worshipped. Then it happened.

When we went into the meeting we enjoyed the atmosphere and the worship, but I can't say that I particularly heard or felt anything from God as we worshipped. Then it happened.

The speaker was introduced, a Scottish lady called Andrea Wigglesworth and as she stood in front of the crowd, she said "God has a word for you tonight, and it's just one word, 'Scotland'". The hair on the back of my neck stood, my heart raced, I started to cry and I immediately knew God was speaking to me and telling me to return to Scotland and give the rest of my life and ministry to this nation and its people. In what was only a moment it was as if time stood still and God spoke a deep calling into me for this land. It would be easy to say that what I heard and felt was due to the emotional state I was in at such a vulnerable time in my life. Or that we were in a difficult situation and this was a possible way out. Or even that I was just hearing what I wanted to hear.

However this was not sentiment and it was not home-sickness. It was for me the actual voice of God, speaking to me. I know 4,000 others heard what I did and I am convinced God will have used that moment to shape calls in other lives too, but I felt I was totally on my own with my heavenly Father. He was so close I could almost feel His breath. Maggie stood at my side, but I honestly cannot even remember her being there at that moment. Some may ask why would God place a call on someone's life for a country they had just left? Others may even correctly ask what right did someone like me have to be even given such a burden in the first place for a country I had moved away from?

> *Why would God place a call on someone's life for a country they had just left?*

Although there are plenty of examples in the Bible and in church history where God did unusual things and called people who were not particularly worthy of that call or who did not particularly want to do what they were being called to, Jonah being one, I am not trying to offer easy answers as to why things happened the way they did. In truth, I'm not sure exactly what the answers to these questions are, but do I know this, that this was a God-thing. Because there was no way I would or could have done what He was going to ask me to do next unless I knew God was in it. The next day at mum's funeral as we stood at the same graveside where my father was buried I knew God was calling me back to this land and I knew we had some hard days ahead.

Shortly afterwards we flew back to Canada and spoke with the church leaders there, sharing our heart and telling them we must return to Scotland. Some understood and some did not, which we accepted. But on 1st September, having sold our house in Brantford, Ontario we were on a plane back to Glasgow and all our belongings were heading back to Scotland on the boat that had taken them to

Canada a few short months earlier. On our return to Scotland we were homeless, jobless, had little money and in some people's eyes even less credibility. We were branded fools by some and failures by others and we did not know what the future held. We only knew that the One who holds the future had asked us to follow him and we had said 'Yes'.

Our friends Gordon and Ann Cowan gave us the use of their static 7-berth caravan in Portpatrick, near Stranraer to live in and Gordon helped get me a car. So where do you begin with a call to a nation when you're jobless and living in a caravan? Well in an amazing way it started as God re-opened the door to the ministry of Word and Sacrament within the Church of Scotland and even more incredibly took us back to lead Oldmachar Church.

The leadership of Oldmachar were unbelievably supportive and I will always be grateful to them for this, especially the Session Clerk Bill Smith and his wife Sylvia who stood with us shoulder to shoulder as they had often before and would do many times again after this.

John Chalmers from The Church's Ministries Council, Ian Maclean, Clerk to the Presbytery of Aberdeen and Norman Smith Convenor of the New Charge Development Committee who oversaw the church's ministry at that time, were all just as encouraging and supportive as the local leaders in what for them was not a run of the mill vacancy procedure. Although understandably I had to go through a rigorous process of interview and testing of this second call to the church, I was in the end once more inducted to the charge of Oldmachar on 5th November 2004. Fireworks night indeed!

We were back in the same church, living in the same manse, with all the kids back at the same schools! There were, of course, those who saw the whole episode as one big mistake and that I had come back from a failure with my tail between my legs. But incredibly none of this really moved me, for I knew what I knew and I knew that if no-one else ever understood, my Father did and He was pleased.

In church we had often sung a worship song which has the words, *'Jesus I believe in You and I will go to the ends of the earth for You'* [vii.] It's easy to sing those words, but it is not just as easy to live them, for they will cost you. However, overall the general feeling from those in the church locally and nationally was really supportive and many said, 'We didn't want you to leave in the first place, so we're delighted you're back!'

As I began the next phase of ministry at Oldmachar I had the distinct honour of being the only person in the history of the Church of Scotland who had both succeeded and preceded himself. Now get your head around that one!

Over the next months and years we picked up where we left off, but also started to move in a new direction in the church and look at new ways to continue to grow and develop the ministry locally, whilst still praying into this sense of how we might follow this call to play our part in what God was doing in the nation.

> *This call back to Scotland was not just to a local church or a city, but to the whole nation.*

About two years after the night in the tent at St. Andrews, Maggie and I travelled down to Edinburgh to meet Andrea Wigglesworth. We did not know her at all at that point but we wanted to share what God had done through her willingness to listen to Him and speak what He said and we just wanted to thank her.

As we shared our heart Andrea was very encouraging and affirming. Then we prayed together before we left. As we prayed God used Andrea to speak into our lives once more and reminded us that this call back to Scotland was not just to a local church or a city, but to the whole nation. As she prayed for me particularly, she again spoke words which blew my mind and seared my heart.

---

vii   From the song 'To the ends of the earth' from Hillsong Music

She reminded me that God had indeed called me to Scotland and said "Jim, I see God giving you a new name. He is writing it on your forehead, he is calling you 'Son of Scotland' " Two years on, those words from God had all the effect that the first one in the tent had.

Naturally I know there is nothing particularly special about me and there are many Sons and Daughters of Scotland out there; many whose lives are sold out to God and to His plan for this nation in this time. Some know it and others are yet to discover it! But all the same those words were destiny shaping for me. I knew who I was, I knew why I was here and I knew how I would spend my life. No matter how anyone else saw me, God saw me as His son and had a wonderful call on my life for this nation He loves. Now I just had to wait for the next part of that calling to be revealed.

CHAPTER 3: HEART BURN!

'Did not our hearts burn within us while He talked with us on the road and while He opened the Scriptures to us?'

LUKE 24:32 NKJV

I had never been to Stornoway on the Isle of Lewis. I had heard of it and my Scottish geography was good enough to know roughly where it was, off the north-west coast of the country, but on one level that was about it.

However, I also knew that this Island had a wonderful Kingdom history. I had read before of the Lewis Revival which had occurred between 1949 and 1953 and had once listened to a recording of the Rev. Duncan Campbell, the leading figure God used in this move, speaking of what had happened then.

As Maggie and I boarded our Eastern Airways jet to fly to the island for a weekend conference I was both looking forward to seeing a part of Scotland I had never been to before and genuinely excited at what God might do on this trip. When I say excited, I should also add, slightly nervous. You see, the jet we were flying on was extremely small and it was a *very* windy November day.

We flew from Aberdeen airport and as usual we were running late. I'm not going to name which one of us had made us late, but suffice it to say it wasn't me. As we hurried through the departure hall, literally running, to our gate, I noticed that the planes got smaller the closer we got to our gate. By the time we reached the gate we would fly from, we were met with this tiny little thing that looked to me like a bath-tub with wings.

The only flying thing I could ever remember seeing that was smaller than this, was the Acme rocket that Wylie Coyote used as he tried to catch The Road Runner. As we boarded the plane I did check for a giant rubber-band at the back of the plane, just in case Eastern Airways was using Wylie's method of propulsion! Thankfully it had some engines, but boy were they loud! When we arrived in Stornoway Airport I was half-deaf, but relieved I was still alive and now full of anticipation for what lay ahead. We were met by the conference organiser, Rev. Tommy Macneil. Tommy was the newly inducted minister of Martins Memorial Church in Stornoway, former minister of Barvas on the island (the same charge as Duncan Campbell) and leader of the 'Stand in The Gap' team who were hosting the conference weekend.

It was 6 months earlier that I had been invited by Tommy to come to Stornoway to speak at this conference. I had been in Edinburgh at the time, taking part as a Commissioner in The Church of Scotland's annual General Assembly in May 2006.

It was just after the session led by the Ministries Council where I had spoken briefly urging the Assembly to consider a radical programme of church planting and new mission initiatives, to have confidence that the Gospel still had the power to save and transform our nation's communities and to get out and go for it. To my surprise it was quite well received!

What I shared was partly in encouragement to the national church of how God had moved in the church plant I was leading at Oldmachar, which was by now a large and ever growing church which was making a real impact in its local community. Yet it was also part of the overflow of my heart for Scotland and my firm belief that Oldmachar was not an anomaly where growth was happening. I was sure that God was doing new things. I remained convinced that this was God's intent for the whole nation, and that what people in Scotland were saying 'no' to was not Jesus, or faith, but the type of organised church we had been offering them.

That was often the case with the hundreds of real people I met and engaged with around the community in which I lived and

I was sure that God was doing new things.

ministered, from the school-gate, to the side of the football pitch, to the supermarkets, hairdressers, gyms and pubs. They were almost always spiritual people, who knew there was something more. Invariably they had no problems with Jesus, but didn't get what church was, or what it had been the last time they had engaged with it. It often gave me such a rush to get them to church or to an event we were organising and see their huge eyes amazed at what they saw and hear them say, 'I just didn't know church could be like this!' I felt that Oldmachar's story was evidence that a relevant contemporary expression of church which actually got involved in the life of a community and its people really can make a big Kingdom impression. My belief was and is that the more we did this the more we would see happening.

> 'I just didn't know church could be like this!'

After the session I went back to Rainey Hall, in New College for a coffee and I picked up a handwritten note from my pigeon-hole (all Assembly Commissioners are allocated a pigeon-hole where notes can be left for them to keep them up to date with each day's debates). It was not the best handwriting I'd ever seen, in fact it was a bit of a scrawl and obviously written in a hurry. But it was signed with a name I had heard about quite a lot in the last year or so, one Tommy Macneil. I was therefore curious and read it right away. Tommy's note simply shared a little about the conference they were holding in November and asked if I would like to come and speak at it, as he'd been encouraged by the passion I had for Jesus and for our nation which he had heard on the Assembly floor.

The minute I read the note I remembered why I recognised Tommy's name. He was the guy that I had heard people from my church rave about after they heard him preaching at a Clan Gathering meeting. I remember thinking at the time, 'He must be a good preacher, for these folk come here every week and they know what good preaching sounds like!' Now that I made the connection

I knew I had heard of Tommy quite a few times. He was someone with whom I was constantly told I had a lot in common and would love to work with.

Whenever he was mentioned, the phrases 'passion for Jesus' and 'passion for Scotland' were inevitably used to describe him, so he was all right in my book. I went home from the General Assembly fully intending to be heading for Stornoway in November.

Needless to say, like all parish ministers, I was always busy and often felt consumed by the local calling I had. I never had to scratch my head to think of what to do next. The next thing always came to me first, particularly so in a growing church planting situation. Because of this I did not manage to accept many invitations to go to speak and minister elsewhere, so despite my real enthusiasm to accept Tommy's invitation, initially I put the note on my filing system, or 'piling system' as I call it and got on with what I was doing locally.

However, after a couple of e-mails from Tommy to remind me of the invitation, I agreed to go to Stornoway and put the dates in my diary. The time passed quickly and now I had arrived. The *Stand in The Gap* Conference had been running for a few years and is led by a local group of inter-denominational Christians on the island who all have a passion for Jesus, a desire to see their island won for him and to see the church transformed to reach today's world. They are all people who are not stuck in the island's past revival history and are longing to see the new thing God wants to do on their island today. They are people of their time. It should also be said that they are people who live in one of the most religious islands in Scotland.

Lewis has only just had its first petrol station open on a Sunday and there is an on-going battle to stop Sunday ferry crossings and preserve a traditional Sabbath, which the traditional church there is fighting to maintain. I do not live there and make no value judgements on this whatsoever. But it does give a picture of the culture in which the islanders live and work, which is so different from the mainland.

To try to do a new thing in this environment, those involved in *Stand in The Gap* have to work with grace and humility amidst some real constraints of the kind I did not have to even think about in Aberdeen. They have had quite a few barriers to break down between what the church is and is seen to be in the eyes of the un-churched on the island and what they long for it to be today.

> *The conference delegates had a good laugh when I confessed my mistake.*

The Conference in November 2006 was entitled, 'Hearts on Fire!', a wonderful title for such a conference if ever there was one. Unfortunately for some reason I got it into my thick head that it was called 'Heart-Burn', which is nearly the same, although with some obvious differences! The conference delegates had a good laugh when I confessed my mistake.

However, it actually made for a very interesting play on words, as I remembered the two men who walked along the Emmaus road with Jesus after His resurrection and later as they recounted their story they said, *'Did not our hearts burn within us while He talked with us on the road and while He opened the Scriptures to us?'* (Luke 24:32 NKJV)

Over the weekend, therefore, I felt my job was to help those present discover or re-discover that burning heart for Jesus and desperate desire for His presence and His word that these men on the Emmaus road had. I even prayed at the end that the whole conference might have a life-long case of Jesus-inspired heart-burn! I still pray that prayer for the Christians on that island and for the church in our nation.

Stand in The Gap '06 was a powerful conference and an inspirational time for Maggie and me on a number of levels. It was a time to make some wonderful new friends not least Tommy, his amazing wife Donna and their two children Joanne and Matthew, whom I am glad to say I thrashed in a late night game of 'Buzz' the interactive TV quiz!

We made an instant connection with the Macneils knowing they were kindred spirits for such a time as this: people who shared the same heart for our land and the same spiritual D.N.A.

Tommy was indeed all that I had been told he was, a powerful preacher and a man of unashamed passion for Jesus and Scotland. His prayers are a thing to behold and are better, more interesting and at times longer than most people's sermons! I have only ever heard two other people like this whose prayers have more heart, emotion, theological truth and spiritual richness than a series of sermons; Eric Alexander, the former minister of St. George's – Tron Church in Glasgow and Abi Tomba, an African pastor from Congo whom God brought to work with me at Oldmachar.

Donna Macneil is quieter than her husband, but has a real ear for God. She hears him, because she spends so much time in His presence, listening to His voice. Then what she hears she shares with a wonderful gentle humility but also with a great prophetic power. She's just like my own Maggie, a quiet Godly woman, a great mum and a great wife, beside and behind a louder, more up-front husband, but who is without doubt his real strength.

It was also a great time to be ministered to by my fellow conference speaker, Rev. John Macleod, a native of Harris now ministering in Newmilns in Ayrshire. John's ministry over the weekend was a tremendous encouragement to us and he has much to share with our nation too. The bonus was in finding that John was a fellow Glasgow Rangers FC supporter, and we had a lot of fun over the weekend as Tommy somehow manages to support our local rivals, that small team over the city called Celtic.

A few months later, a local Stornoway businessman, Innes Macleod, who had recently come to faith through the ministry at Martins Memorial and who had been blessed by the conference took John and me to Ibrox to share his hospitality as a thank you for our ministry over the weekend. It was a fabulous day during which we met some old Rangers legends and we had first class treatment all round. Rangers were playing Aberdeen and won the match 3-0 thanks to a Kris Boyd hat-trick and after the game I drove back to my home in Aberdeen with a nice smile on my face. Naturally, I was not smug at church the next day!

However, more than anything, the weekend in Stornoway in November 2006 was a timely reminder of my heart for the whole nation of Scotland and my conviction that a new thing had to happen here and indeed it was beginning to do so. One particularly interesting moment came when Tommy and Donna took us to see Barvas church where Tommy had previously ministered and where Duncan Campbell had preached during the 1950's revival.

On one level it was fascinating to stand in the place where thousands of lives were touched in a peculiar way by God and where a whole island had been impacted by the work of Spirit of God. It was encouraging to realise that if God could move in a wee church in the middle of nowhere like this then He could move anywhere. Therefore even my ministry, which is totally insignificant in the great scheme of things, could see unusual favour like once was seen here. Strangely though, it also felt eerily cold and empty. At the end of the day all I felt was that here was a place where something had happened once, but that was a long time ago. That's not to say that the church in Barvas are not loving or serving or worshipping God there any more, of course they are! Nevertheless, I felt that there was no sense of magic in the place itself. All the power was in the One who made it happen, and He hasn't got stuck like often we in the church have.

> *It was encouraging to realise that if God could move in a wee church in the middle of nowhere like this then He could move anywhere.*

There are no holy places or holy people without the living, moving presence of a Holy God. And there is no golden age or holy past that has forever gone to the church of today with only reminiscence left as we ponder what once was but is not anymore. I was also reminded that God is not sentimental about the past and He is not tied to a building or a particular time. After all He allowed The Temple in Jerusalem to be destroyed. You would think that if there was one building He would have a vested interest in keeping intact it would be The Temple.

Neither does He do encores. He will not simply replicate what once was. He does not hand out old manna, for after a while it goes off and is useless. He is far too creative to be stuck in a pattern or a place. His grace and mercy are new every morning! This means that those who travel the world to see where God once moved in a particular way, like in Barvas, or those spiritual surfers who chase the next wave, wherever that may be happening, or go seeking out the next 'big name' who is bound to bring God with him or her to their city, are actually wasting time if the 'experience' alone or the sense of history is all they are seeking. They would be better off spending their time seeking to find out what God is doing now amongst their own community and join in! He is surely working there already.

History can teach us a lot and it is good to know how God once moved and there is something exciting and encouraging in going to see, or reading and hearing how God is moving in different places around the world today. I have done this and will do it again. But not as a 'revival tourist', as an investment in the place and people God has called me to.

I am desperate to see Him move here in Scotland in radical new power today.

For nothing can possibly compare to the joy of seeing God move in our life and in our community now. If I am honest I am weary of hearing how God used to move in Scotland or how He is moving in other places around the world in amazing ways. I am desperate to see Him move here in Scotland in radical new power today.

The evening following our trip to Barvas I was speaking at a Praise Night in Martins Memorial Church Hall at the part of the

Conference that is opened up to Christians from all across the island, whether they are conference delegates or not. The hall was packed and the praise was exciting and inspiring. I had something prepared to share, but during the worship God led me to completely drop that and share something different. Preachers reading this will know how scary it is when He does that! I felt that God simply wanted me to encourage them to keep going with what they were doing and to let them know how pleased He was with how they were seeking Him and reaching out on the island. Yet more than that to tell them that this was their time. They were not to be held-back or haunted by the ghosts of the revival that had been. They had not to try to replicate or re-discover what happened 50 years ago. God was about to do a new thing with them. Duncan Campbell's time had been amazing, but this was their time and what they would see in the days ahead would be every bit as amazing for their generation.

God was about to do a new thing with them.

As we travelled back to Aberdeen in our flying bath-tub, I reflected on the weekend. It was a real blessing that my ministry had been so well received and that I was able to encourage people to go a bit deeper and seek God a bit more and maybe I did have something to share beyond my own parish. More significantly than that, it wasn't what I could see God doing through me, it is what I could see God was doing in people right across our land from the north to the south and the east to the west.

If I could go to Stornoway on the Isle of Lewis and see God moving in power in a new way today on such an island with all its religious constraints and possible restraining historical legacy then surely it could happen anywhere in the nation. If there were people like this on a wee island at the top of the country with such a 'heart's on fire attitude' towards God and His mission to Scotland, then they must be everywhere in this land. I couldn't wait to discover some more of them.

CHAPTER 4: SEND ME

Then I heard the voice of the Lord saying, 'Whom shall I send and who will go for us?' And I said, 'Here am I Lord, send me!'

ISAIAH 6:8 NIV

I used to be quite troubled when I heard Christians speaking about 'hearing' from God, or when people said 'God told me... (*this or that*)'. What did they mean? Was it an inner sense of direction that was so sure they knew it was God? Or were they claiming to have heard an actual audible voice from heaven?

I often mused, 'Could they not be put away for claiming that?' It seemed to be as peculiar as claiming to be Superman or Napoleon! It was all a bit troubling for me. This was mostly for one reason and that was that I had never experienced it. That is usually where our theology either stands or falls on an issue, has it happened to us?

I was also very suspicious of the 'prophetic' and by that I mean those people who said they had a 'word' from God for themselves, for someone else, or perish the thought, for me! I can remember one very bad experience when a well-meaning, but slightly misguided charismatic Christian whom I didn't really know, pulled me aside after a meeting and said he was sure he had a word from God that I had a 'spirit of lust' and needed to be delivered from it and publicly confess to this. My response was as moderated as it got in those days, as a 17 year-old football player from Airdrie who had not long become a Christian and for whom sanctification was a process which was a long-way from being completed. I stopped short of a Glasgow-kiss[viii]. Just short!

---

viii A 'Glasgow kiss' is a head butt!

The truth is I was 17, had hormones flying all over the place and like any normal young guy at that time in life, I definitely did have some work to do on the old lust department, but this man and his clumsy way of bringing this 'word' to me was not how I was going to deal with it. Consequently, for a long time afterwards I felt the whole prophetic/word from God thing was for the flaky nutters of the

> *The truth is I was 17, had hormones flying all over the place*

Christian world like him and I avoided it and them, like the plague.

Don't misunderstand me, I believed the Bible, every word of it, and I knew God did lead us and spoke to us through His written Word. As the Psalmist says, *'Your word is a lamp to my feet and a light to my path'* (Ps 119:105 NIV). And as Paul says to Timothy, *'All Scripture is God-breathed and is useful for teaching, rebuking, correcting and training in righteousness'* (2 Timothy 3:16 NIV) I also believed in prayer and the sense of leading one gets when a prayer dialogue with God appears to have a very direct end result. I knew God spoke in that way. All of this had been part of my Christian walk since I became a believer.

I had become a Christian as a teenager in Caldercruix Parish Church of Scotland, just outside Airdrie, a great little church where I heard who Jesus really was, gave my life to Him, learnt to pray and was, over the years, taught God's Word faithfully by the ministers there. This is also the place I began to develop my life-long passion for mission and evangelism. Encouraged by the leaders there I headed off, as many a young Church of Scotland member has, to be part of the Church's Summer Mission programme. From 1980 to 1982 I had some wonderful times as part of teams; one in Campbeltown and two in Peebles.

The real bonus happened in Peebles in June 1982 when I met a beautiful young Christian woman called Maggie Taylor. Incredibly Maggie also lived in Airdrie, although we didn't know each other. I later discovered that she even stayed right next to my uncle and we had apparently played together as kids when I was visiting my cousins, but we couldn't remember that. But perhaps it's good we properly met when we did, as Peebles is a tad more romantic than Airdrie and it was at the side of the River Tweed that Cupid shot a very accurate arrow into each of our hearts. We fell in love, got engaged 3 months later and were married on 3rd September 1983.

In between our engagement and our wedding we both knew we wanted to give ourselves to God's service. We enrolled to study theology at The Glasgow Bible Training Institute in preparation for whatever ministry God opened up to us. After Bible College and our wedding we got involved in full-time ministry and have been doing it ever since. It has been a many and varied walk, mostly wonderful and rewarding, often immensely difficult and usually we have been totally skint, but somehow provided for by our faithful God and some of His generous children!

> *In between our engagement and our wedding we both knew we wanted to give ourselves to God's service.*

I have worked as a youth worker in Glasgow and in Troon; as lead singer/songwriter of '80s and early '90s Christian rock band *Triumph* (legends!) and as a minister and pastor in churches in Perth, Aberdeen and of course briefly in Brantford, Canada. Not forgetting a five year period of study at New College, Edinburgh to complete the two theology degrees required by the Church of Scotland to enter the ministry.

At the time of writing this book that's 26 years of full-time ministry and theological study and as you would expect, a few things have changed over the years. Hopefully there are many ways in which I have grown as a Christian and in my understanding and relationship with God. One of the areas that has developed most, is my understanding of how God *does actually* speak to us personally and to my surprise I came to realise He *had* in fact been speaking to me and I had been responding to His voice all of my Christian journey. Even better, I came to find with great joy that He also actually did speak to me very clearly and directly too, and I was indeed 'hearing' His voice.

To my delight I have, like many before me, come to realise that hearing God's voice is not at all flaky, irrelevant or condemnatory. It is natural and necessary and as essential to our spirit as air is to our lungs.

It is powerful, yet gentle, incredibly relevant and always immensely encouraging, even when He is rebuking and correcting. All of which are truly authenticating signs that a word is from God [ix]. Over the years, as I have walked with God and as I have read His Word I have realised that it is not possible to believe every word of the Bible, as I supposed I did, and yet reject the prophetic ministry as 'all just for the nutters'. In fact the flaky-ones have done the Lord, His Word and the church a great disservice, by side-lining the prophetic to this extent. For that reason I am glad it is now being re-claimed in mainstream church life as much as it is by mature and relatively sane church leaders!

For it is not something for the strange few, but a gift from God for all His children which is so ingrained in how God communicates to us, in both His written Word in Scripture and the Living Word His Spirit speaks to all who have an ear to hear. This was powerfully re-affirmed to me recently when I was speaking at 'Islands Ablaze' conference in Orkney. One of my fellow speakers, Dr. Jonathan Oloyede, a Nigerian-born Pastor who leads the Glory House in London shared his own story of how he came to faith in Jesus when as a Muslim student some Christians took him to a prayer meeting. Jonathan said he had been a very devoted Muslim all his life but for all he prayed five times a day he had never heard Allah speak back. He was desperate to hear the voice of God, and at his first ever prayer meeting with Christians he heard Jesus speak to him and he responded in faith. He says God has spoken to him every day since!

ix   See 1 Corinthians 14;1f

My understanding of the prophetic has come alive both as God has spoken to me in fresh new ways and as mature and gifted Christians with a beautiful prophetic ministry have spoken words to me which connected to my soul and spoke life into my heart. My moment in the tent at Clan '04, and then with Maggie in Andrea's Edinburgh office would not have been so life-changing had I not known that this was truly God speaking and that I was open to hear from Him.

> *I have been richly blessed by members of the body of Christ who have come to me with real words God had given them for me and this has really built me up.*

There have been times when God has spoken to me when I was desperate to hear from my Father, and there have been times when He has spoken to me in wonderful, yet much more unexpected ways when I hadn't even asked Him to speak. I have been richly blessed by members of the body of Christ who have come to me with real words God had given them for me and this has really built me up, unlike my first unfortunate experience of a 'word'.

Also, God has given me real words for others that I have been able to share in my pastoral and preaching ministry and these have been as encouraging to them as others' words have been to me. And I've not even gone flaky in the process! Hearing God's voice has become central to every decision I have made as a Christian and a church leader, especially at critical points of my life and ministry when the direction ahead had to be made clear.

There have also been times in my life and ministry when I have been struggling or under pressure when all that has kept me going was a word from God over my life, either one He had given me directly from Scripture or one spoken to me by a brother or sister in the Lord.

If you are reading this and are currently in a place, maybe a very hard place, where you are holding onto nothing but a word from God, I want to really encourage you to hold on and don't give up, for as God says to Habakkuk, '*If it seems slow in coming, wait. It's on its way. It will come right on time*' (Habakkuk 2:3 TM). As you wait, wait and hope in the Lord, and He will renew your strength [x] for whatever you are going through and waiting for.

After hearing the 'Scotland' words from God I treasured them in my heart as I ministered at Oldmachar and although there were many days when I had no clue about how this might all work out, I knew that they were from God and in His time He would fully reveal what they meant and how they would show themselves in my life.

In the summer of 2007 there was a quickening in my heart and something was beginning to move in my spirit that a new time was coming in my ministry. As I read God's Word He continually challenged me that a new thing was coming and that my time at Oldmachar was drawing to a close. In particular as I read John 3 one day I felt God quite clearly say that just as John the Baptist had to 'become less' so that Jesus would 'become greater' , so must my ministry in Oldmachar decrease in order that Jesus'

> *There was a quickening in my heart and something was beginning to move in my spirit that a new time was coming in my ministry.*

ministry through others might increase there. A few months later I was speaking to a group of friends about my sense of being called on to something new and I shared this sense I had had from John 3. One of those present, Kenny Borthwick, shared that some months earlier he was speaking to a member of Oldmachar in a completely unrelated conversation about the church and as my name was mentioned Kenny got this exact same word from God in John 3 about my ministry decreasing in Oldmachar.

Along with this sense of 'decreasing' in my local ministry I was being given more words of direction from God about 'expanding' my own territory, in particular from Isaiah 54: 2, '*Enlarge the place of*

---

x   See Isaiah 40: 31

your tent, stretch your tent curtains wide, do not hold back; lengthen your cords and strengthen your stakes' (Isaiah 54:2 NIV) There were growing feelings within Maggie, myself, our two older daughters Pam and Dawn and some of our closest friends that a releasing from local to national ministry was coming soon. In June I was on study leave and the purpose of this month away from parish duties was to pray and reflect on where Oldmachar might go next as a church.

Oldmachar church had been planted by a core group of 12 people and now there was a critical mass of around 400 in the worshipping congregation, as well as a separate local schools and youth ministry through a trust we had set up called *The One Trust*. This was reaching out to around 10,000 young people a year. To lead all of this we now had a staff of 12 on our ministry team. The church building was getting regularly filled to capacity on Sunday mornings and we had been looking at options which would increase the capacity of the worship space including a possible building expansion programme. Consequently, I went off to look at churches that had grown over that 400 mark and at different models of church which had a similar missional ethos, but on a larger scale. I read books, prayed, met people, reflected and wrote a bit.

But over that month as I prayed for Oldmachar I continually got the same picture of a great future for the church, but without me in it! During this study time we were blessed as a family to be able to go on holiday to Cyprus for a couple of weeks, again thanks to our friends the Cowans, who had traded in their seven-berth caravan in Stranraer for a 3 bedroom villa with a pool near Ayia Napa. As good a trade as I think is possible! O.K., I know it's not going to sound much like study, but at the side of the pool I read and prayed every day and the same thing came to me from God, 'It's time to step out from Oldmachar and give yourself to me for whatever I want to do through you in Scotland.'

I returned to work at Oldmachar in July and from that point on I knew I would be leaving, even though I wasn't sure when or how. I was not unsettled or unhappy, more impatient to hear a clear call from God with all the detail I was looking for. Normally at the end of the summer I would present numerous visionary ideas to the ministry and leadership teams at Oldmachar and I would be buzzing with what would come next for the church. But this late summer and autumn were different. I felt God leading me to just be faithful in what we were already doing and wait on Him.

In September I was at a Heralds Trust Leader's day in Aberdeen with Luis Palau. He is a fabulous character with lots to share and many great anecdotes from his days as a world-renowned evangelist. However, two things from that day really stuck with me. Luis told a story of how he first moved out of his job in a bank to minister in Argentina. He knew he was to become a full-time minister but was waiting on a clear call. One day his mother was telling him of a town nearby where there were lots of opportunities to minister but with no evangelical church there to do so. She said, 'Why don't you go there and start reaching out for Jesus?' Luis replied, 'I am waiting on a call'. To which his mother replied with exasperation, 'A call, a call! The call went out from Jesus 2000 years ago. He's just waiting on people to take it up and go and do it!' Luis said that moment was life-changing for him and he left the bank, went into ministry, and the rest, as they say, is history.

Hearing this I was really challenged by God to stop waiting for all the details of my call to become clear and just to go and do it! On the way out of the conference, Luis was at the back of the hall at a table signing copies of his latest book and speaking to people. As I walked out past the table he beckoned me in, shook my hand and said, 'You're the evangelist'. He then turned back to what he was doing. I have never met him before and he had certainly never heard of me. Was this some more direction from God as to what I was to be about next?

A few weeks later I was visited at my home by another incredible man of God, Emmanuel Ziga, whom I have only met four times, but every time I meet him he speaks into my life with real clarity. Emmanuel is from Ghana but now leads a world-wide ministry to encourage pastors and church leaders, called 'Grace for all Nations', which is based in Seattle, USA.

I was first introduced to him by my friend from Aberdeen, Brian Taylor, who has introduced a number of amazing people to me over the years and has been a real source of encouragement to me to be all I can be in my life and ministry. Brian called to say that Emmanuel was in town and wanted to see me. When we got together he said he knew there was a new call on my life and it was for the nation. He said God wanted to increase the extent and scope of my ministry, and that this was my time to give myself to Scotland! Blown away again by God's goodness to encourage me in this way I fully shared my heart with Emmanuel and sought his prayer and counsel. He went on to share some amazing things with me, which I will keep to myself as they are personal words for me that I will hold on to and treasure when the going gets tough.

All over the world people have been waiting for Scotland to rise up again. I am so excited. Heaven rejoices. This is your time!

But there was one thing in particular he said which really impacted me. He said, 'All over the world people have been waiting for Scotland to rise up again. I am so excited. Heaven rejoices. This is your time!'

One morning in late October Maggie and I were talking and praying in the manse conservatory and as always the conversation was coming back to what I might do next. Maggie said that it was time to just trust God, step down from Oldmachar and let God lead me on to the next chapter of our lives and ministry. I explained that I had no problem with all of that, but had no idea how to do it practically and was scared. If I did this I would have to leave Oldmachar, step out of the salary structure of the Church of Scotland, which is not extravagant, but pays the bills and more importantly we would have no manse, and nowhere for the family to live.

I had been hoping and praying that God would do it all the easy way for me, by giving me some 'miracle' money; enough to get us a house and give me a salary to just go out and do whatever God called me to. But this was not happening, and was not looking as if it would any time soon. So for me to give it all up and just trust God was terrifying, especially with a

> *For me to give it all up and just trust God was terrifying, especially with a big family to provide for.*

big family to provide for. I told Maggie that to do so would be 'like jumping out of a plane without a parachute'. Despite all the words and encouragements I felt we were no further forward.

The next month we were back in Stornoway. A year had passed since the last *'Stand in The Gap'* Conference and I had been invited back to speak on this year's topic, 'Lost'. It was great to see Tommy, Donna and all the Stornoway team again and I was delighted that my co-speaker this year was going to be Andrea Wigglesworth. On the Friday night when we were together for the first night of the conference I told Andrea that on the two previous occasions I had been in her company (granted the first one was along with 4,000 others), she had spoken words which had changed my life. 'No pressure', I said, 'but I hope you can keep it up!'

On the Saturday of 'Lost', I was speaking at the first session, to be followed by Andrea. My topic was 'Here am I, send me'. I spoke about hearing God's voice and the urgency to respond to His call. It was quite ironic really, as this was the thing I was struggling with most at that moment. But no-one knew that except me, Maggie and the Lord.

I also spoke of how we were witnessing Isaiah's destiny moment in his call, recorded in Isaiah Chapter 6 and I encouraged the conference to trust that God has great plans for all of our lives and that each of us has destiny moments, which if we respond, will not only change the course of our lives but the lives of all those God is calling us to go to. There was a good response to this word and I felt that God had spoken to people. We had a coffee break and then Andrea was up for the next session.

As she stood to speak, she said she would not be able to start her given topic yet, as God had given her a specific word to share first.

"This is a destiny moment, a life-defining moment, for someone here today"

She said, "This is a destiny moment, a life-defining moment, for someone here today" and she looked at me and said, "It's for you Jim, would you mind standing up?" Maggie and I stood together and Andrea started to speak what she felt God was saying to me. The first thing she said just about had Maggie and I on the floor; 'Jim, the Lord says you have to jump out of the plane, but He will provide the parachute'.

It was hard to remember all the rest of what Andrea said, as I was overwhelmed and un-done by God. But I remembered the main points and thankfully the rest was captured by the sound guys for the conference CD set and I listened back to it all later. I'm glad this was recorded and that there were a couple of hundred witnesses present, as there was no way I could have just been hearing things!

Andrea said that God was calling me from an old ministry to a new one and one which was not just about a local church, but for the whole of Scotland. I was to go out and call people all over Scotland to 'destiny and life-defining moments'. She said that it was God's plan for my ministry and its scope to grow and expand. She likened this growth in my life and ministry to a new suit of clothing, the sort of growth which takes place as a boy becomes a man and becomes too large for the suit he once wore. He then needs a bigger suit.

This new suit, she said, was a suit I had never thought I could fit and that I had believed it was for someone else, but it was not it was purpose-made for me. God knew my heart, He knew my insecurity and He knew I did not feel able or worthy to take on what to me felt a calling that was a bit too big, and a bit too difficult to make happen. He was telling me this was His call for my life, and that He would make it happen.

As Andrea was speaking Tommy came to stand beside me and after Andrea had prayed Tommy then shared an equally encouraging word God had given him for me along similar lines. Andrea resumed her teaching session, which was, as always, inspiring and then we all went for lunch. As we left the conference venue to go for lunch I met two friends in the car park, Innes and Finlay who were still excited about what had just happened. Innes said, 'I feel privileged to have been in at the birth of something new for you and for Scotland'.

When I returned to Aberdeen after the conference, I was going to jump out of the plane.

Over lunch a few of us shared our sense of anticipation of what was to come and all agreed that this was indeed a life-defining moment for us and prayed that it was part of a new time for Scotland. Suitable to the occasion and to make it all feel like the official start of something new we all toasted Scotland with glasses of our other national drink, Irn Bru!

I knew there was now no going back and when I returned to Aberdeen after the conference, I was going to jump out of the plane.

CHAPTER 5: THE SCOTLAND TRUST

Making God's name great! God making our nation great!
'Righteousness alone exalts a nation'

(PROVERBS 14:34 NIV)

When I looked at my diary I could hardly believe the date on which the meeting was to take place.

I had come back from Stornoway buoyed up by God in what I was to go and do and had started the process of speaking to the people I needed to, to make the way for me stepping out of Oldmachar and into this new calling, whatever it would look like.

To start with, I set about arranging a meeting in Aberdeen with half a dozen close friends from around the country, with whom I would share my heart and ask them to stand with me in this next step. These were all people I looked up to in Kingdom terms, whom I knew and loved and whom I believed would support me in this calling, if they knew it was of God, as they were all kindred spirits. But crucially they were all very capable people in their own right to whom I could be accountable and who would not just tell me what I wanted to hear.

Three of those I had asked were going to be in Aberdeen over the weekend of 30th November to 2nd December, so it made sense to meet then. Tommy and Donna Macneil and Kenny Borthwick were to be in the city for a Conference in Sheddocksley Baptist Church that weekend, at which Kenny and Tommy were the keynote speakers, so I had asked which day suited them best during that time. Tommy called to say that a breakfast meeting on the Friday was best for Donna and himself and that he had spoken to Kenny who could also meet at that time. I therefore decided on that day and time and prepared to e-mail the arrangements to the others.

When I put the phone down and went to write the date in my diary I noticed in the top right hand corner of that day's space it was printed, '30th November, St. Andrew's Day'.

We were about to meet for the first time to prayerfully birth what was to be a new ministry to the nation, which we would call The Scotland Trust, on St. Andrew's Day. In case you don't know, St. Andrew's Day is the feast of Saint Andrew, celebrated on 30th November each year. Saint Andrew is the patron saint of Scotland and St. Andrew's Day is Scotland's official national day. In 2006, the Scottish Parliament designated the day as an official bank holiday. Now if you're Irish then you know that 17th March is St. Patrick's Day and half the world will celebrate it with you. But in typically under-stated fashion we Scots have never made as much of St. Andrew's Day as we should. I think that will start to change now that the Scottish Parliament has made it a bank holiday. However, that's why when we were speaking of a date for our meeting we did not automatically notice the significance of that date. Nevertheless, I believe God knew and was making a statement of intent to us.

What He had put in our hearts to establish was indeed to be an important part of this nation's future for Him. I will forever remember what day 30th November is now. So on St. Andrews Day 2007, The Scotland Trust was born. The heart of the ministry would be demonstrated in our vision statement; *'Making God's name great! God making our nation great! Righteousness alone exalts a nation'* (Proverbs 14v34 NKJV)

> *What He had put in our hearts to establish was indeed to be an important part of this nation's future for Him.*

The name, The Scotland Trust, had come to us on the road from Lewis to Harris the day after Stand in the Gap '07 had finished. The Macneils were taking us down to the Isle of Harris for some sightseeing and lunch before we flew home that night. In the car we spoke of how the weekend had impacted us and shared stories of what God had done in people's lives. Of course, what God had spoken to us on Saturday was high on the agenda. That day in the car and over lunch we talked, prayed and dreamed some dreams. We felt led to come up with a structure which could release me to minister as God called me to and at the same time administer and financially support this new work, therefore giving both some creative freedom as well as a means to facilitate a new ministry.

We felt that a charitable trust, with trustees, a board of management and a respected council of reference was the most sensible way to administer the new ministry. Tommy suggested the name, 'The Scotland Trust', which we all immediately knew ticked all the right boxes; for this was not about the ministry of Jim Ritchie, but a ministry for Scotland and to Scotland. We went back to Aberdeen in our wee toy plane and although it was once more windy and bumpy it was one of the best flights I have ever been on. It could have flipped over and come into Aberdeen upside down for all I cared. I had a special peace in my heart at that moment, which nothing could destroy. For I knew God had placed a new destiny in my life. He had said, *'Whom shall I send and who will go for us?'* And I had replied, *'Here am I Lord, send me!'*

> He had said, *'Whom shall I send and who will go for us?' And I had replied, 'Here am I Lord, send me!'*

In the weeks after returning from Stornoway running up to Christmas, I shared what God had asked me to do with the core leaders of Oldmachar, the senior members of my ministry team, the Presbytery of Aberdeen and the national church. This was not an easy thing to share with those I worked with and led at Oldmachar as these were all people I loved and had been through a lot with. Telling them I was leaving them was hard. Yet I had given all I could to the church and to get to where we had over that time was neither easy nor cheap. It was very costly to me personally and to all of us as a family.

There were times, when like all pastors, I had walked a thin line between busyness and burn-out, as well as many times when I went to one more meeting, or to try to sort out one more difficult pastoral situation, when I was not with Maggie or the children. For just under eight years I had poured my heart, soul and all my energy into leading and building up a new church. Some of the things I had had to do as a parish minister I would not miss, those were things which had never really been within my personal gifting and had always been on the edge of my comfort zone. So whilst I really looked forward to what would come next, I still knew it would be difficult for many in the church to hear that I would be leaving them.

A few days before I began this process, Maggie and I were again praying in the conservatory and I was sharing with her and the Lord how I was not looking forward to possibly hurting people I loved, no matter how excited I was about what would come next. As we prayed God again spoke to me in a beautifully reassuring way, like only He can. God is so good. His kindness to the smallest detail in our lives is amazing and shows His unique Father's heart to us, even although we never deserve it.

The Saturday when Andrea had prayed over me at the conference, Tommy had also shared some specific words God had given him too. He said that the 'suit' Andrea had seen God giving me was a very special kind of suit. He said it was my own personal 'rocket suit'! He said that God had reminded him of a movie he had once

> *As we prayed God again spoke to me in a beautifully reassuring way, like only He can.*

watched with his kids where a man had a rocket suit that allowed him to fly into space on his own. Tommy said that my calling would require me to hear God in ways in which I had never heard Him before and that I would then share what I heard with others throughout the land. Also, He would take me higher than I had ever been before, to hear Him and then bring back what was on the Father's heart to share with His church. Tommy said he saw my calling as a very personal 'rocket man' calling on my life.

These words are also captured on the conference CD, and when we came home I let the kids hear the whole thing. They were all really excited at what God said to me, but also had a chuckle at this picture of their dad with a rocket suit on! Now, as we prayed in the conservatory some weeks later, I asked God if He would just encourage me before I went to my colleagues to tell them I was moving on and confirm that this was indeed the right thing I was doing. I had not lost confidence in the calling, I guess it was just a Gideon moment when I was needing some reassurance [xi]. I remember saying in prayer 'Please speak to me right now Lord'.

> *I had not lost confidence in the calling, I guess it was just a Gideon moment when I was needing some reassurance.*

At that exact moment my mobile phone bleeped, telling me I had received a text message. It was from my daughter Dawn, a fantastic singer who had moved to Bristol to pursue her career in the music industry. Her text was sent from Bristol city centre. The exact words of the text were, *'Hi Dad. Just going into a theatre in Bristol, and there is a huge billboard next to the theatre with a man in a rocket suit, and the words 'Rocket Man' underneath him. I've no idea what it's for but just felt I should tell you I saw this. Speak soon, luv Dawn'*

Once more amazed, I knew that this was God speaking in a very unusual but highly personal way to remind me this was all His idea and to reassure me to keep going. I phoned Dawn to tell her about this and explain how amazing the timing was, to which she replied, 'Well it's going to get even more amazing, because I wrote that text an hour ago and tried to send it to you 3 times, but for some reason each time the text wouldn't send. It was only the fourth time of trying that it went to you, just when you needed it!'

An hour before that we were not praying and I had not asked God to speak to me. If the text had been received then, it would have been interesting, but would not have had the effect God clearly desired it

xi   See Judges 6 and 7

to have. I have been in ministry for a long time and as a Christian I have been to a lot of places and have seen a lot of things. You could say I've been around the block. I am not naive and can be as cynical as anyone. So when I've read books before and heard stories like these I know the temptation to see co-incidence, and people reading things into a situation that are not really there. You just have to trust me. This is what happened and it was no co-incidence.

This encouragement allowed me to go with confidence to all those with whom I needed to share the news that I was moving out of Oldmachar to a new calling with a national focus. My friends on the church's leadership team were all very understanding and fully supportive, although personally sad that my family and I would be leaving Oldmachar and the Presbytery of Aberdeen and those whom I spoke to at a national church level were equally supportive.

My colleague Abi Tomba was as inspirational as always when he heard the news. He had tears in his eyes when Maggie and I told him, yet immediately shared that he knew this was of God. In fact he said, 'This is an answer to prayer for the church'. I know Abi loves me and would not mean

'This is an answer to prayer for the church'.

that getting rid of me was an answer to the church's prayers! He went on to remind me that in November and December of 2005 when our church had 50 days of concentrated and intentional prayer, we had cried out to God to use us not just to reach our local community, or our city, but the nation as a whole. As a church we had prayed, 'God use us to reach Scotland'. Abi smiled and said, 'God is now answering our prayer and sending you out for this purpose'. I guess this is a lesson to us all to be careful what you pray for as God may just give it to you!

In early January 2008 I shared my heart with the congregation of Oldmachar and over the next 6 weeks we prepared to leave these people we loved, to go on this new adventure. Throughout that time we were totally overwhelmed by the complete support of our church family who were determined to help us leave well and truly send us out for this cause. It was also affirming to receive dozens of emails, letters and calls from friends and colleagues around the country who, when they heard the news, contacted me to offer their support and give their blessing to this new calling. It was humbling to hear many say that they felt this was the right call for this time and I was the right man to do it.

Our last Sunday at Oldmachar Church was Sunday 24th February and it was a great day for us all, particularly as our whole family were together in worship for the first time in a few months. Dawn had been in Bristol since September and then our oldest daughter, Pam, an artist, singer and dancer moved there after Christmas to take some time out and give herself to God and hear His voice for her life.

As we stood on the front row of the church; Maggie, Pam, Dawn, Andy, Becky, Gavin and me, I knew we had all given our best as a family there and we had always tried to do as the Father had asked us to. I was content. I knew we would leave a gap, even physically as there are a lot of us! But I was excited for the church that some of them would now step forward to do things they never knew they could and that in time someone else would come and have their own unique ministry there.

At morning worship one of my last acts as minister of Oldmachar was to ordain as an elder a dear friend, Sandra Hutchinson. Sandra is part of Oldmachar's leadership team and along with her husband John had always been incredibly loyal and supportive to us and the family, especially as we returned from Canada in 2004. Then after I had preached as minister there for the last time the church leaders and pastors gathered around us, with the whole church reaching out to us in blessing and prayed us out to this new call.

The final words that morning were spoken by John Swinton. John is Professor of Practical Theology at Kings College, Aberdeen, an ordained minister of the Church of Scotland, a member of Oldmachar's leadership team and most importantly to me, my mate! He read as our commissioning these words from Deuteronomy, *'The Lord Himself goes before you and will be with you, He will never leave you or forsake you. Do not be afraid and do not be discouraged'*. (Deuteronomy 31:8 NIV)

After a church lunch when we said our goodbyes to as many people as we could we came back for the evening service, which, fittingly was also a baptismal service where 6 teenagers were to be baptised and publicly proclaim their faith in Jesus. We had always done things differently at Oldmachar and when there were adult baptisms each year I always used a large tank for full immersion baptisms. The church loved it done this way and it was

> *'The Lord Himself goes before you and will be with you, He will never leave you or forsake you. Do not be afraid and do not be discouraged'*

very special for those being baptised. Many family members, often non-Christians, would come and see what was going on and the incredible symbolism of dying and rising again to life in Christ right there before their eyes in a huge tank, could not have been so powerfully portrayed with just a wee sprinkle from a font! The adult baptisms were always in every way events in themselves. With the poignancy of this particular day this one was even a little more significant than normal for me.

The first few times we had a baptismal service we went to our friends at a local independent church, Oasis Christian Fellowship, to use their baptismal tank. Pastors Neil and Fay Smith were always welcoming in allowing this. But eventually I wanted our own tank. We couldn't dig up the floor to put one in, although I did ask! Hence, I asked two of my leaders, Ian and Andrew, who were D.I.Y. experts, if they could build us a portable tank which we then erected in the centre of the sanctuary and filled with hundreds of gallons of water once a year for our own baptismal services.

Apart from one famous occasion when the hose-pump emptying the tank burst and flooded the place we had no real mishaps and as I reassuringly told each candidate for baptism every year, no-one had ever drowned on me! That night the church was packed, the atmosphere electric, and it was a great way to close this chapter in our life and ministry.

So on Sunday 24th February 2008 at 8:30pm after two truly inspirational times of worship, having given and received more hugs than I could remember, with slightly heavy hearts but also with the real joy of belonging to something bigger than ourselves, I walked out of Oldmachar Church's front door for the last time as minister of that congregation. One door had been closed by God. It was now up to Him to open the next one.

CHAPTER 6: CAN I SEE SOME I.D. MR. RICHARDS?

---

*'I pray that you, being rooted and established in love may have the
power to grasp how wide and long and high and deep the love of
Christ is, and to know this love that surpasses knowledge – that you
may be filled to the measure of all the fullness of God'*
EPHESIANS 3:18-19 NIV

It never ceases to amaze me just how much God loves us and the
lengths He will go to in order to show us that extraordinary love.
It is incredible that He would do just one thing, which in the universal
scheme of things appears small and potentially insignificant to the
Creator of everything there is, but He does it nonetheless and it has
a profound, life-changing impact on one of His children. I have
experienced this in my own life so many times and as a pastor and
evangelist I have witnessed it so often that it should not surprise me
when I see it in a new situation, but it always does!

As Paul writes to the believers in Ephesus he tries, as only a
preacher can, to explain to them just how marvellous and all-
encompassing that love of God is, in and through His Son, Christ
Jesus. In chapter 3 verses 18-19 Paul prays that the church there
may be able to grasp: *'how wide and long and high and deep the love
of Christ is, and to know this love that surpasses knowledge'*. How
people need to know that this is true. How all the people in our
nation in these days need to see and hear this love demonstrated in
a relevant, practical way and come to see that God loves them and
cares deeply about them and their lives.

During my final weeks at Oldmachar Church, a member of my
fellowship, a dear friend and brother, Jack Fraser, was diagnosed with
cancer and his family were told he only had days to live. Jack's
family are lovely folks and his wife Lily is a real angel, without doubt

one of the most practically loving and Godly people I have ever met. Although she struggles with her own health she loves, prays for and supports so many people in Jesus' name. She is a wonderful cook and uses this gift as a ministry to bless others. Whenever there is a need to be met, Lily is often first on the scene. Over the years Lily has cooked so many lovely meals for our family and for others, just at a time when it was needed most and Jack was her delivery man! When Jack appeared at the door with bags of food you knew Lily had been busy in the kitchen. More than once as we struggled to the end of the month for the next pay cheque and prayed that God would help us and meet our needs a food delivery from Lily would be cheerfully dropped off by Jack.

Typically, Lily was the first person who connected with us when we moved to the church. On the night before I preached as sole nominee at Oldmachar, for the congregation and ourselves to decide if this was indeed God's calling, we were staying in a Travel Inn in Bridge of Don in preparation for the next day. When we arrived at the hotel we were given a card and a bunch of flowers by the receptionist which had been left by Lily for this family she had never met, but whom she wanted to make feel welcome and to know the peace and assurance of God's call in a strange place.

We became very close during my time as minister at Oldmachar and Maggie and I spent many hours with her in hospital wards, beside her bed in her frequent stays in Aberdeen Royal Infirmary. Lily always views her time in hospital as an opportunity to love someone and be there for someone who needs her and who of course, needs Jesus. Often when I arrived for a visit she would tell me who it was God had brought her in to hospital to love this time.

On a few occasions when I was about to pray with her in the hospital before leaving, Lily gathered all her room, or half the ward, round for prayer, often including staff. Had I asked them to gather round for prayer they would have looked at me as if I was crazy, but such was Lily's witness that they all came for her without any problems. She would get everyone to hold hands and then she'd say, 'Right Jim, you just pray for us all now'. No pressure! On one other famous occasion she managed to persuade the ward staff that she needed a day-pass to come to Oldmachar for church on Sunday morning and she arrived with 2 nurses and 3 other patients in tow, all in wheelchairs and with oxygen canisters in hand. God did a mighty work in their lives that day.

Lily and Jack supported us when I lost my parents, and after my mum died Lily came to me and said, 'I can't replace your dear mum, but until we get to heaven and she can take over again, I'll fill in for her'. And she has done ever since. Jack's faith had really come alive during an Alpha course that we held in the church. He was a quiet, practical Christian man with a lot of love and a dry Aberdonian sense of humour. Now Jack and Lily were in a place that they had supported us and others through many times, as they walked through the valley of the shadow of death.

> *I had my Bible with me and asked the Lord to guide me as to what to read and when to do so.*

The night Jack died, the family were all with him in Roxburghe House Hospice and I got a call to go and be with them. As we sat around the bed talking, I had my Bible with me and asked the Lord to guide me as to what to read and when to do so. I felt Him say, 'You'll know the right words and you'll know the right time and Lily will too'. So I waited and listened. Then when I felt sure it was the right time to read, I looked at Lily and she said to me, 'What do you have for us from God's word Jim?' I began to read Psalm 23.

As a minister I have read and sung this Psalm at a family's request at so many funerals that I confess that sometimes, the power of the words and the great hope and promise they bring can be a bit lost due to their familiarity.

So Psalm 23 would not usually be my first choice of scripture in such a situation. However, this time it was different and I knew these were the right words to read. As I read, Jack visibly relaxed and his breathing slowed down. Then as I spoke the last line, 'And I will dwell in the house of the Lord for ever', Jack breathed his last and went home to be with Jesus. This was as peaceful a final moment as I had ever seen and God's timing in it all was just extraordinary. The last words Jack heard in this life were an assurance that he would live with the Lord forever in the next and the first face he would see was the face of the One who had made him that promise. What a comfort this was to him and to all his family gathered there! This moment of God's tender love had a profound impact on us all.

Jack's funeral and thanksgiving service was the last one I conducted at Oldmachar church as minister. As I shared this story of how God had been there with this family as their Good Shepherd, to a packed church, I believe some people heard for the first time or had re-kindled in them the reality of this all-encompassing love of God that is wider, higher, longer and deeper than we can ever imagine.

On the first day of my new calling with The Scotland Trust God showed me this again and in an incredible way reminded me just how much He loves people and the unbelievable, even unusual, lengths He will go to show them that He does. We had just moved house, which is an awful experience in itself and I was not particularly calm and serene. In fact, I was stressed and positively grumpy. I had done all the usual jobs one must do in moving home; notifying everyone of our change of address from the bank to our car insurers, giving final readings and first readings to the electricity and gas suppliers in both homes, the one we had just left and the new one we had now moved into and cancelling our British Telecom (BT) telephone line in the manse and getting a new one ordered for the new house. It was BT who had put me in a bad mood.

I was stressed and positively grumpy.

I had spent quite a while on the phone before we moved telling them we were moving, giving our new address and ordering a broadband hub to give me internet connection as soon as possible in our new home. On the day we arrived, we just missed the postman and he had left a card saying there was a package for us at the local collection depot which I could go and pick up. It was a package for 'Mr. Richards'. There was also another letter waiting for us from BT and that too was addressed to 'Mr Richards'. I therefore put two and two together and guessed it was my broadband hub that the postman couldn't get through the letter box which was at the collection depot. I wanted this as soon as possible, since like most of the modern world I am now unable to function without e-mail, so I set off to get it. Of course my name is Ritchie and not Richards and as I drove to the post office I was muttering away to myself about me being a BT customer for 25 years and despite me having just spent an hour on the phone speaking to different departments organising the details of this move they still couldn't even get my blooming name right!

I arrived at the collection depot, went in, handed over the card from the postman and asked for my package, to which the man behind the counter replied, 'Can I see some I.D. Mr. Richards?' After a moment's stunned silence as the situation began to sink in I tried to explain to this guy that I wasn't Mr. Richards, in fact he didn't exist, but that he had a package for him that I needed, because actually the package was for me! Not surprisingly he wouldn't give it to me.

About an hour later after a run home and then back to the depot, the post office worker finally accepted that this was my package and I got my broadband hub. Immediately, I was on the phone to BT, totally fed-up and not particularly patient, to complain and get them to change my name on their records. Again I was transferred from department to department, with what seemed like an eternity on hold in between and finally got put through to a call centre in Pakistan or India. The call centre worker asked my number and what the problem was. When I told him all about the wrong name situation, he said he couldn't deal with that but would transfer me to someone who could. After another long hold, another man came on the line and said, 'How can I help you Mr. Richards?' This was officially the moment that the final straw broke the camel's back and the poor man on the other end of the phone got the full force of the irate ranting of a guy from the west of Scotland. Of course it wasn't his fault and thankfully he couldn't understand a word I said. Eventually, after I had explained the problem and spelled my name to him three times, he promised that it would be sorted.

On a couple of occasions during the whole episode Maggie tried to tell me not to get so uptight about this and just forget it. But I'm afraid I was like a dog with a bone and wouldn't let go. So, as she does, my patient wife went and made me a cup of tea at the end of my ordeal.

As I sat there starting to feel a bit calmer and slightly guilty for getting so angry at complete strangers I heard God speak to me. He didn't give me the ticking off I probably deserved, He simply said, 'That's how many people in the world feel. They feel as if they don't exist and don't matter to anyone. They feel as if no-one even knows their name. To the world they are nobodies who can't even get hold of the things that they should have by right. No-one seems to either care or do anything about it and they're unable to get anywhere in life. They're hurt, lost, angry and fed-up. I wanted you to know what that feels like and to go and find these people and tell them I know them, I know their name. It's written on my heart.

> *That's how many people in the world feel. They feel as if they don't exist and don't matter to anyone. They feel as if no-one even knows their name.*

I love them and they matter to me'. I was humbled and a bit ashamed, but grateful to God for this lesson He had taught me.

That night I went off to speak at my first ever engagement with The Scotland Trust. I was to be the speaker at a monthly dinner event held in a hotel in Kirriemuir organised by friends there, Kenny and Lynn Gillies. I had prepared a talk on Ephesians 3: 18-19 about the extent of God's love and as I drove down the A90 I thought and prayed through what I was going to say that night.

As I did, I felt God encourage me to share the BT episode of that morning and afternoon and what He had taught me through this because there would be someone there who really needed to hear this. Consequently, I did as I was led and explained, right at the start of my talk, what had happened earlier that day. I got some laughs as well as some sympathy from folks who have been in similarly frustrating situations. But I also shared what God had said to me through it and said, 'I believe there is someone here who may need to hear this'. At the end of the night, as people were leaving, a young woman came to speak to me. She had tears in her eyes and was clearly moved by something that had happened or had been said. As she spoke to me she explained that she was a mother of six who had been coming to church on her own with her children and had made a commitment to Christ but was now struggling to keep going. She said that she was about to give up on God. She had not intended to come to the dinner, but had eventually decided to give it all one last chance. Her problem was that she felt that 'she didn't matter to God or anyone else, that no-one even knew who she was, including God, and her life was not important to Him'. But now she knew that God knew her, that He loved her, that He was interested in her life and that He 'even knew her name'! It amazed her that God would send me all that way to share this story with her just to let her know that He knew her, He loved her and that He always will. I prayed with her and was so thrilled to be there as she made a fresh start with Jesus and committed her life to Him for good.

> *She had tears in her eyes and was clearly moved by something that had happened or had been said.*

I had gone to Kirriemuir to preach on the extent of God's love and in the process had seen God show me what that love looked like in real life. How wide, how long, how high, how deep. How awesome.

Driving home that night, I was amazed that our loving heavenly Father would let me go through all that hassle and allow me to get so upset with something as irrelevant as an internet hub and a phone company just so that He could tell a young mum that He knew her and He loved her. I continue to pray for that young woman and for her children, that her decision to go on with Jesus will transform their lives and destiny. And, yes, I will also always be grateful to BT and Mr. Richards for their participation in this wonderful little God moment that I experienced on the first day of my new ministry with The Scotland Trust.

I continue to pray for that young woman and for her children, that her decision to go on with Jesus will transform their lives and destiny.

CHAPTER 7: POWER TO LIVE

*'Lord our hearts cry out for freedom for the captives of this world,
that their bondage may be broken in the name of Christ our Lord.
May they know the true salvation that only you can give, give them
hope and liberation and the power to live'*

When I saw Alastair come into the church during worship and go straight to Maggie I knew something was wrong. From the front of the sanctuary I could see everything that happened in the open-plan glass building we worshipped in, so when Alastair, a member of our church and one of the dads from Andy's football team, came rushing in during the service to speak to Maggie and she immediately went out, I knew that Andy had been hurt. I tried to look composed and in control, but inside I was churning and was desperate to somehow find out what was wrong. Thankfully it was right at the end of the prayer before I let the children go out to their own teaching time, so as our musicians played and the children left, I was able to quickly walk out to the foyer to find out what had happened.

> *I tried to look composed and in control, but inside I was churning and was desperate to somehow find out what was wrong.*

My two sons Andy and Gavin are great footballers, as well as being boys who know and love Jesus. It was a tough decision for us as a family to allow them to play football for their Aberdeen Juvenile football clubs on a Sunday, but as our church in Oldmachar had so many other opportunities for them to worship and fellowship, including Sunday evenings, we felt we should let them play.

In making the decision Andy, who was 11 at the time, pulled the trump card as he said, 'Mum and Dad, God gave me this talent to play football and I want to use it for His glory'. After this it was a done deal and we let the boys play on Sunday mornings with their clubs, Andy with Lewis United Youth, and Gav with Dyce Boys Club. Then they came to worship with us all as a family in the evening. So each Sunday dads from their teams would drop the boys off after their games and they would usually appear at the end of morning worship in their strips, covered in mud.

On this particular day, when Alastair appeared without Andy, after what would have been only 20 minutes of their game it was obvious that something was not right. When I spoke to him, he confirmed my fears, 'Andy's been hurt. He may have broken something and he's in a lot of pain. They've taken him to hospital'. Maggie left immediately and I went back into the sanctuary to preach and lead the service to the end. I prayed quietly for Andy, committed him into God's care and continued with church. I trusted the Lord, but my son was hurt and whatever was going on, his pain really hurt me too.

> *I trusted the Lord, but my son was hurt and whatever was going on, his pain really hurt me too.*

When I arrived at the hospital, Andy was being very brave, but he could not walk and was clearly in pain. His left foot was very swollen and he was taken for an x-ray. Nothing was broken, but he had badly torn his ankle ligaments, an injury from which it would take him three months to fully recover. Andy's injury was a normal sports injury. It was not life-threatening or serious in any way to his long-term health. Even so, it caused him a lot of pain and because, as his dad, I love him, his pain really mattered to me. The Accident and Emergency staff were wonderful and strapped him up. They were so busy and understaffed that they were waiting for a wheelchair to get Andy to my car to take him home. I told them not to worry. I would carry him. As I carried my brave but hurt son to the car on my back, he leaned forward and quietly spoke into my ear, 'Thanks for carrying me Dad. I love you'.

I've thought of that moment many times since and of how many broken people there are out there who have been hurt, damaged by the world and who need to know their Father loves them and that their pain causes Him pain. They need to know that He will come running to them and if they will just let Him, He will carry them. These are people whose lives are as torn as Andy's ankle ligaments were, and like his foot that day, they cannot take the weight of their life and so their world collapses.

I have been in that place in my life too and I know that sometimes no amount of self-help talks or encouragement will do. Unless someone picks you up and carries you, you are going nowhere. I have also been with others many times in these broken moments and I am convinced that the church needs to do two things with the hurting people who are all around us: let them know that they have a Father who hurts because they hurt, and then actually take them to this loving Father who will bear their burden. We need to carry them to Him ourselves, if necessary. Like the four men in Mark 2 who carried their paralysed friend to Jesus and ripped open the roof of the home He was preaching in to lower this friend they clearly loved right to the feet of Jesus. For me, that is one of the clearest examples of what church should be to those around us and if we were like that more often how different the world's view of us would be.

> *The world often sees the church as a disempowering body, which in their eyes is judgemental and wants to stop them from really living.*

The world often sees the church as a disempowering body, which in their eyes is judgemental and wants to stop them from really living. Of course, this could not be further from the truth. The church is the body of Christ in the world whose calling it is to go to the world and actually empower them to *start* really living the life God always intended them to live – a life lived to the full and a life that Jesus died to give them. The church has to become known as the visible face of Jesus, His hands and feet in the world who, like Jesus, will show people what God really looks like and how much He really cares. Then when they are broken they will know where to go to. We need to be the spiritual Accident and Emergency departments in our communities and we need to be the human stretchers or wheelchairs that will carry the broken and hurting to a Father who loves them and cares.

Many churches struggle with falling numbers coming to their services and often wonder how they might get people back into church. There are loads of books which give possible answers, techniques and programmes which may or may not help. However, I think we need to start by simply loving our communities in Jesus' name by going to where they hurt and letting them know that God is with them and for them and so are we. This practical demonstration of God's love will earn us the right to be part of their lives and speak into them once more. Over the years it was one of my greatest privileges to see the people in the community around Oldmachar church come to realise this was our heart and to know that we were always there for them. I could share many stories of this, but one in particular stands out.

> *We need to start by simply loving our communities in Jesus' name by going to where they hurt and letting them know that God is with them and for them and so are we.*

One Sunday morning I had gathered in our ministry room before the service to pray with the worship team as we always did prior to leading worship. As we prayed I could hear loud sobbing coming from the foyer. I left the prayer room to go and see what was happening and saw a young lady in the arms of Lily, crying her eyes out. This broken hearted girl had just heard that there had been a tragic death in her family, a suicide, and although she had never been into the church before, she knew about us and had heard we were people who cared, so this was the only place she could come to. We comforted her as best we could, then we prayed with her and she stayed for the service. After worship was over I spoke to her again and she asked if I would conduct the funeral which would have to take place and come and meet her family. I agreed to do both.

The next evening I went to the address that I had been given, to have the meeting about the funeral. I had expected there to be two or three people to be in attendance as is normal at such a meeting, but was surprised to find the whole family, three generations of them, crowded into the living room. The young woman who had come to church the previous day had gathered all of the family together to meet me and she wanted me to share with them what I had said in church on Sunday. She said it had really helped her and she wanted me to share this hope she had found with them all. This poor family were devastated at their loss and were clearly looking for whatever comfort they could find at such an awful time.

> *This poor family were devastated at their loss and were clearly looking for whatever comfort they could find at such an awful time.*

As always in these situations in which we can find ourselves as Christians, the first thing to recognise is that God is already there working and that He loves the people we are meeting in His name. I felt His real compassion for them and as best I could I shared my heart with them about Jesus' love for them and the hope that God can give, in and beyond death and tragedy. I can remember being told in Pastoral Care lectures at university of the danger of transference and about getting too emotionally involved in pastoral situations and how being detached is essential to protect the pastor. I've never been good at that. Since my first pastoral visits as a student, I have always found myself laughing with those who laugh and crying with those who cry.

As I met with these broken hearted people to share my heart, I also felt theirs. We cried, we laughed, we prayed and clung on to the hope that only Jesus can give. That night was the beginning of a long relationship and friendship with this family. The girl I had met at first and her younger sister, who both lived nearby, started coming to church regularly and in time both came to faith in Jesus for themselves. I have also had the privilege of being with them all again through another family illness and bereavement, as well as in happier times in baptisms and weddings. Through it all, they came to know that God's love and God's power and God's people were for real. This, for me, is the power of the Gospel which is totally unique. It is a power that heals and a power that transforms and it is all the work of Jesus. All we need to do as a church is to get close enough to people for them to know we're there and that we care and God will do the rest.

All we need to do as a church is to get close enough to people for them to know we're there and that we care and God will do the rest.

I believe this is where the church's impact can be not only life changing, but community transforming. Despite everything that this humanistic, materialistic and individualistic world we now live in would say, I believe that people are still desperate to find something more, that they want to feel they belong, they want to believe in something, they want more than they currently have and not just in a material way.

If only the church would realise that we have what they are looking for, what their soul yearns for, and that in Jesus the answer to all the world's longing is still to be found. If only we would have confidence in the redemptive power of the cross and the reality of the resurrection, worked out in the everyday lives of real people today to bring hope, comfort, joy, peace, purpose, fulfilment and a life worth living with a future that is secure. As Paul says, *'For I am not ashamed of the gospel of Christ, for it is the power of God to salvation for everyone who believes'* (Romans 1:16 NIV). Or as the Message translation puts it; *'It's news I'm most proud to proclaim,*

*this extraordinary Message of God's powerful plan to rescue everyone
who trusts him'* (Romans 1:16 TM)

A number of years ago, whilst leading a youth outreach in Airdrie
and Coatbridge called 'Power to Live', with my friend Jim Stewart, I
wrote a song which became the mission theme-song. The chorus
says: *'Lord our hearts cry out for freedom for the captives of this
world, that their bondage may be broken in the name of Christ our
Lord. May they know the true salvation that only you can give. Give
them hope and liberation and the power to live'.*

My cry at that time was for the young people of the Monklands
area, in the schools and communities there who had been
disempowered by life and the circumstances around them and for
some of them often entwined with teenage alcohol and drug
abuse, violence and social problems that seem well outwith the
church's reach. Our conviction then was that the gospel of Jesus
was still the answer and still had the power to reach and transform
everyone and everywhere.

This mission made a tremendous impact in Airdrie and
Coatbridge and some of the lessons I learnt then were seminal in
the youth and schools work I would later
pioneer in Aberdeen and believe could create
change all over our land. The words of that song
are still my prayer for the people of Scotland
and for all those who are disempowered by life,
inside and outside the church. My desire is for
the church to cry out with passion and expectation to God for the
captives all around us and then go out in Jesus' name to set them
free. Also, for those who are bound, often with chains they cannot
see, to come face to face with the living Son of God in the face of
His people as they love and serve them in His name.

> How I long to see a church that isn't bogged down by church!

However, for that to happen, the church itself needs to be set
free. How I long to see a church that isn't bogged down by church!
Not held back by religion, tradition, structure, inner-conflict,

programmes, past failure, self-doubt and fear. In the pre-flight safety instructions passengers are always reminded that if oxygen is needed we have to put our own mask on before we try to help others. I think that at times, the church needs to take a deep breath of God's air supply and breathe in the breath of freedom itself before it can begin trying to help those around.

Don't get me wrong, I don't think the church in our nation is all bad or ineffective. There are many faithful people all over the country doing great things in Jesus' name in all sorts of places and in many denominations. As I've said in previous chapters, I am excited at what I see emerging in the church in Scotland. Nevertheless, I still believe we are not all we could be and we could be so much more. In my time at Oldmachar I often felt this for myself and my own ministry.

> *I am excited at what I see emerging in the church in Scotland.*

Even amidst our 'successes' there was still a sense of frustration in our 'failures' and a sense of the enormity of all that was still to be done. Some of this was real, as the road back from irrelevance to relevance amidst three and four un-churched generations was a long one. But some of it was not real. It was the chains of self-doubt and restrictions that were of man's and not God's making. The freedom cry is as desperately needed for the found as it is for the lost.

This was very vividly, and very movingly, shown to me at the 'Islands Ablaze' conference in Orkney in April 2008. During one of the morning sessions as we worshipped, God powerfully and tenderly came to us as we were singing. Local Orcadian singer and worship leader Michael Harcus, a very gifted and anointed man, was leading us and we were singing the song 'Eagle's wings'. As we sang, I felt such a growing desperate longing within me for me, and the church in our nation, to be as free as the eagle we were singing of. Then Bert McKaig from *'Pray for Scotland'* came to the microphone to share a story from one of the 50 days he had spent walking around Scotland praying, the previous year.

During his 50 day prayer walk he had stopped off for a comfort break with his team. Outside the place they were going into, he saw an exhibition of birds of prey and noticed an eagle. It was tied to a post by its leg and unable to fly off. Bert asked his team what they could see, and they said, 'a bird!' But he said, 'What I can see is a picture of God's people in Scotland. They are bound and restricted, tied up, and not free to fly as they were intended to'. Bert said that he had once heard that the eagle was the only bird that could fly whilst looking straight at the sun. He reminded us all at the conference that as God's people we were not made to be tied down or bound by anything, but we were made to fly high and free, always looking at the Son.

The amazing thing is that the things that tie us down and hold us back as God's people were never meant to and they don't have to for one moment longer if we refuse to accept them. If we simply choose to be free in Christ, then we are and if we refuse to live any other way we can be the bearers and bringers of freedom to all who are bound around us.

'For if the Son has set you free you are free indeed'. (John 8:36)

CHAPTER 8:
'IT'S CHURCH JIM, BUT NOT AS WE KNOW IT!'

*He said to me, "Son of man, can these bones live?" I said, "Master
God, only you know that." He said to me, "Prophesy over these
bones: 'Dry bones, listen to the Message of God!' "*

EZEKIEL 37:3-4 TM

I am not a 'Trekkie' (a Star Trek anorak for those of you who don't
know what that is), but Peter Lloyd, one of the Leadership Team at
Oldmachar church, is. During the years we were building a culturally
relevant church there and usually going against the flow of what was
around and what was expected, Peter often gave a lovely little twist
to a quote from Star Trek which perfectly described what we were
trying to create. In one of the episodes of Star Trek on yet another
galactic adventure, on discovering a strange unknown life form,
Spock says to Captain James T. Kirk, 'It's life Jim, but not as we know
it'. For those of a certain vintage, you may remember both the line
itself and how it was immortalised in the cheesy 80's pop song 'Star
Trekkin' by The Firm.

On reflecting on some of the things we were doing and how
different they were from what may have been expected of a Church
of Scotland parish church, frequently when I had come up with
another idea which was about to take everyone even further out of
their comfort zone, Peter would say, 'It's church Jim, but not as we
know it!' He was right of course. What we were doing, and what I
felt God push us ever onward to create, was nothing like what
anyone would recognise as a local parish church in the North East
of Scotland. But nonetheless it was church; church as I saw it lived
out in the New Testament and church as I felt it needed to be for
this time in history. It was church as I was convinced God was
inspiring it to be for us. To further continue on the Star Trek theme,

I was sure, as all pioneers in ministry are, that we were to 'boldly go' to where we had never been before. Whether anyone else had ever done it exactly this way before was totally irrelevant.

I have often asked people who don't go to church, particularly younger people, what they think of it. Most of them have no personal experience to help them to judge, only their perceptions and those perceptions are often of an irrelevant relic of the past that has no particular place in their life, nor in the life of modern Scotland. By and large, most people in the street seem to me to have no interest in the church as they see it. Equally, over the last 15 years, I have seen people in the church in our nation gradually lose confidence that there is any likelihood of the church turning things around so that it becomes a transformational influence in society or of it placing itself at the heart of its community. We therefore accept a peripheral role and a marginal influence. To many people in Scotland, both inside and outside the church, the feeling is that the church is either dead or slowly dying.

I have often asked people who don't go to church, particularly younger people, what they think of it.

So in building this new church I had been called to, the place where I felt God wanted us to boldly go was a place of relevance, a place of contemporary influence and a place where we fully engaged with the world and the people around us. It had to be a place where people had not only to know that we existed, but one where they knew exactly what we were about, for we were making a difference to the world around us in Jesus' name. I believed we were to be 'the head' and 'not the tail'[xii]. I refused the possibility that we could be seen as an oddity or an irrelevance to those around us and refused to allow us to be ignored.

However, I am not purporting that we should all have a vision of a triumphalistic, imperialistic church that simply has influence and

xii   See Deuteronomy 28:13

power and does nothing good with it. On the contrary, we must be the Kingdom church the Bible describes, that reaches the heart of everything around it, which cannot be silenced, will not be bridled or tamed and in every way turns the world upside down (or right side up, as the case may be). For I am convinced that that is what the Lord requires of us. I love what God says through Micah, *'What does the Lord require of you but to do justly, to love mercy and to walk humbly with your God?'* (Micah 6:8 NIV). These are not the attributes of mere passivity and they do not apply to a church that is irrelevant. This is dynamite, which blows the world's minds and changes everything around us.

You cannot act justly if you do not know where the injustices are in the world *you* live in. Neither can you show mercy if you do not know the people who are in need of mercy. Unless you can speak in a language the people around you can understand, there is no conversation to be had with them. If we walk humbly with God, that in itself is so radically different from the world values our society treasures, that we are bound to be noticed at the very least! People may not always agree with us or want to be like us but they will know we're there. Yet many will find us irresistible, as the life of Christ living through us touches, attracts and fascinates them.

> *You cannot act justly if you do not know where the injustices are in the world you live in. Neither can you show mercy if you do not know the people who are in need of mercy.*

In order to achieve all this, I knew we had to be a truly contemporary church and by that I do not mean 'youthy' or 'trendy', but simply relevant to the time and place in which we lived, because to make the kind of influence we need to make, irrelevance is not an option. I had been in plenty of churches that were relevant to the 1970s or 80s, in some that bore more relation to the 1950s or 60s and a few that would have struggled to be contemporary in the late 19th century!

I could have pulled my hair out when I spoke to church leaders who claimed to be contemporary in their expression of worship, but by the millennium had only just discovered 'Shine Jesus Shine'[xiii]. So how do we get to this place of local cultural relevance from a place of irrelevance, lack of influence and almost terminal decline?

Ezekiel was given a vision by God, recorded in Ezekiel 37, which may well be appropriate and prophetic to the church in our land in this time. The scene God allows him to survey is of apparent death with no sign of life. What Ezekiel sees is a graveyard. But what God sees is an army! A living army, which with one word from Him can get back on to its feet and with one puff of His breath will come alive and be a mighty army again. This is an awesome vision and one I hold on to dearly for the church in our nation in these days.

For Ezekiel to see that pile of bones become a mighty living army he had to see things as God saw them; imagine what was possible with God; do the things God asked of him in faith and then leave the rest up to God Himself. Of course, the story tells us he did all of this, the army rose and new life sprang up all around. The same can happen for the church in Scotland, indeed for the church all over the world where it is dead or dying. Remember, God specialises in resurrection after death! Therefore there is hope, even in the cemeteries and morgues we can sometimes find ourselves in.

> Remember, God specialises in resurrection after death!

It is also about our perception. We can bemoan the fact that we are in the church in our land at the time when it is at its lowest ever ebb and therefore most difficult to sustain or maintain and as a result of that, we completely modify our hopes and expectations. In doing that, the best we may do is have a stab at resuscitation, or if we don't think that is possible, just come up with some life-

---

xiii 'Shine Jesus Shine' written by Graham Kendrick,
Copyright © 1987 Make Way Music

support systems to keep the body alive as long as we can. At worst we can just give up and wait for the inevitable visit from the grim reaper. This was the way Israel saw things at the time of Ezekiel's vision. God said, *"Son of man, these bones are the whole house of Israel. Listen to what they're saying: 'Our bones are dried up, our hope is gone, there's nothing left of us."* (Ezekiel 37:11 TM). Not very optimistic really and in truth the reality of their situation did not give them much cause for optimism. They were a defeated people in exile. As a nation they were as good as dead.

> *We can see this time we live in as an occasion for what God specialises in most – resurrection!*

Yet in such a place it is also possible to see things with different eyes, with the eyes of faith. We can see this time we live in as an occasion for what God specialises in most – resurrection and know that we are in the time of the greatest opportunity for mission that there has ever been for the church in our nation. We can see ourselves on the verge of a turnaround of Biblical proportions, literally! We can believe wholeheartedly that if we do 'prophesy over these bones' and cry out to God to send the breath of His Spirit amongst us again, not only can God's army stand up once more, but the whole nation's fortunes can be turned around. Listen with the ears of faith, see with the eyes of faith and imagine what is in the mind of God. In response to the desperate gloom of the people in Ezekiel's day God said this, *"Therefore, prophesy. Tell them, 'God, the Master, says: I'll dig up your graves and bring you out alive – O my people! Then I'll take you straight to the land of Israel. When I dig up graves and bring you out as my people, you'll realize that I am God. I'll breathe my life into you and you'll live. Then I'll lead you straight back to your land and you'll realize that I am God. I've said it and I'll do it. God's Decree.'"* (Ezekiel 37:12-14 TM).

During the years I was minister of Oldmachar church, I saw the same national church statistics that everyone else saw, I heard all the talk of gloom and read all the predictions of when the church would officially die in Scotland. In my first year of ordained ministry I can remember reading that the church would be totally dead within 10-15 years, which did not say a lot about my long-term job prospects as a 35 year-old married guy with five children! But I also read in God's word, that Jesus promised to build His church not bury it and I heard the voice of God say, 'I've said it and I'll do it'. So my conviction was never to accept any inevitability except that of God and the last I heard God was still fully committed to His church being the transformational body of love,

> Jesus promised to build His church not bury it!

justice, power, grace and new life which He birthed it to be at Pentecost and it still had the job of reaching the whole world and making disciples of people everywhere, before the inevitable return of Jesus to the earth in all His glory.

This then, was always the backdrop to my ministry and my expectations and in eight years there, God never deviated from *His* misson statement once! I got things wrong and made lots of mistakes and when I tried to build *my* church I failed miserably. But when I worked with Jesus as he built *His* church I could see amazing new life everywhere, some of it on a scale that surprised even an optimist like me. Even more so now that I am National Director of The Scotland Trust and I have a heart for the whole land and a commission to work at a national level with the church around the country. I am sure that not only is it possible for us to see things turn around, but I am absolutely convinced of its inevitability. For as I read those words in Ezekiel, I hear them in my heart for Scotland and for the church in Scotland and I know God will turn things around again. Some of the churches may have died, some may be dying and some will yet perish, but after death will come resurrection.

What always fascinates me about Jesus' resurrection as it is recounted in the Gospels, is that those who first saw the resurrected

Jesus were those who loved Him most and had been with Him most, including very recently, and yet they didn't always recognise Him. It appears from the New Testament that His resurrected body was different, but the same! It seems that He had all the qualities of Jesus, but in a new, even more wonderful form.

I guess the New Testament as a whole hints at this and gives us all the expectation of resurrected bodies that give a degree of continuity with what came before, but are wonderfully new and different. When you get to the wrong side of forty and things on your body start to head south or spread out to the east and the west, this is a nice thought!

> The church which emerges in this nation... will have a degree of continuity with the past; ... but it will look new and different in other ways.

So I believe it will be for the church which emerges in this nation. It will have a degree of continuity with the past; it will remain faithful to the core of what it always was; but it will look new and different in other ways. In some ways it will be radically different. I think this can worry some of us in the church more than it ever should. I know it doesn't worry God!

There will not have been a church leader in the country who, in trying to bring something new or different, will not have been greeted by those words from the sidelines that are intended to stop all progress or experimentation in their tracks, 'We've never done it like that before', or 'We've always done it this way'. Those words and those who speak them can be immensely frustrating, but often when I have heard them they have made me secretly smile as well, as the words and those who speak them are so reminiscent of the two crotchety old balcony commentators in 'The Muppets', Statler and Waldorf!

Some will desperately try to cling on to church as we know it and as it's always been and others will resist that which we've never done before, but to do either would be fatal. We should always remember that the church as we know it is as alien to many of the people of our nation, especially the younger generation, as the unknown life form in Star Trek was to Spock and Kirk. We have to create church not necessarily as we know it, or once knew it, but as the people we are called to reach out to will be able to understand it, engage with it and relate to it. Church as we knew it doesn't exist any more and if it does, it won't for long.

> *Church as we knew it doesn't exist any more and if it does, it won't for long.*

Only as church takes the shape, form and context of the time and place it lives in, whilst remaining true to its core message, can its transformative gospel penetrate our communities. Then we will see new life come amongst those who are not alive to God.

The church of Jesus Christ has always been able to do this throughout history and it has to do it again today. What we have to do as a contemporary 21st century church is to know our context, interpret the situation which faces us now and determine how we 'prophesy over these bones', for they are all around us. The church cannot pretend that it is not standing in a graveyard, nor can it just accept where it is, dig a hole and jump in. We have to see the bones, yet prophesy to them believing God will bring the life He has promised.

In Oldmachar church we worked hard to understand who our neighbours were, for it is hard to love them if you don't know them and we always wanted to know what the world around us was all about. We tried to create a faith community that was passionately Biblical, thoroughly evangelical, theologically orthodox, always incarnational, yet in our practice we sought to be cutting-edge, radical and contemporary. Most of all we tried to see where God was working and join in! To me this is the key to prophesying to the bones.

I firmly believe that if we go to the place of greatest need, wherever that may be, we will meet God there. In some communities that will be to the physically poor, the oppressed, the homeless or whoever the broken are. In others, it will be to the addict, the violent and the victims of violence. For some it may be to the rich, the successful, the busy, the powerful and even the corrupt. In our suburb of Aberdeen, we identified the greatest need as being amongst families and school children, teenagers and those hanging around the streets at night. I could see many good kids with little purpose and not much to do, becoming a real handful for their family, their school and for the community at large.

There were also relatively few who had any contact with or interest in the church. The church around them was dead to them. Here was part of our graveyard. So how could we prophesy to them? On becoming minister of Oldmachar church, I also became the chaplain of five schools with a total school population nearing 2,500 children. Here I had been given a massive opportunity to be a contemporary expression of Jesus and His message to these thousands of kids, to their teachers and to their families. I had the opportunity and the responsibility to show them that Jesus and His church were relevant to their lives today.

> I had the opportunity and the responsibility to show them that Jesus and His church were relevant to their lives today.

Initially, I did all the schools work on my own – just me and my guitar and then after a year or so I got some great help, with the appointment of my first full time youth worker Dougie Adam. As time went on, we created a chaplaincy team in the area, with colleagues from all the local churches. Our school assemblies became multi-media presentations with music, dvds, powerpoint presentations and dance and we did four annual Christian focus weeks in our local high school, Oldmachar Academy. At the same time, we developed an extensive programme of events for the young people around our community in the evenings at the church centre. The success of our schools work paid off enormously, as hundreds of young people from our community came every week to the ministries we led. It wasn't always easy to control and it was time consuming and messy, but we were now engaging in a culturally relevant way to very many of the children and young people in our community.

We were starting to make some impact, but I knew there was much more that could be done. Our ministry and leadership teams were always totally supportive of all new ventures as they were presented to them – and my session clerk Bill Smith and I presented many. Bill suggested we have a look at a Youth For Christ

> *We were starting to make some impact, but I knew there was much more that could be done.*

(YFC) sports ministry called *Kick*, which placed a small residential team of trained volunteers in a local church for a year at a time. I realised this was what we needed and we went into partnership with YFC in this and got our first *Kick* team in 2004. They led football and sports coaching and outreach work in schools, local sports centres and the church. I could see doors opening and a pattern emerging where designated resources, plus relevant engagement would produce relationship and local influence.

Gradually, I started to form a vision for how this might expand, not only locally in our community, but city-wide and potentially even nationally. The vision was to have a local Trust set up to fund and administer this ministry within the schools, youth population and families and to have full-time sports and music teams working hand in hand to do so. I saw opportunities in the voluntary work and year-out explosion which was beginning to happen and even the Scottish Executive's Project Scotland scheme, where volunteers could be paid a small amount to work with community projects, seemed to be in our favour.

The vision became a reality in June 2006 when we created a local ministry called *The One Trust* which saw a full-time schools rock band of talented young Christian volunteers being formed to work along with our third *Kick* Team. We called the band, *The One Band* and appointed James Gregory, one of the founders of the

Imagine Festival, to oversee their work on a daily basis. The doors opened amazingly and in the first year *The One Band* played every day in schools throughout the city at assemblies, lunch-time concerts and at after schools gigs. They also did a monthly concert in Craiginches Prision in Aberdeen and helped others in missions around the country.

In the first year, *The One Band* shared a fabulously engaging and contemporary message of Jesus to over 10,000 children and young people locally in around 20 schools. In year two, those numbers rose to 25 schools and 15,000 young people. For all this to happen we had to find a lot of money for full-time staff, accommodation and running expenses. Also, the dynamic of now having a ministry team of 12 people working together on a daily basis certainly kept me on my toes, but it was all worth it. We were prophesying to the bones.

As some of you read this, I believe God will be placing in your heart where your graveyard is in your community, that place where the church is dead, but into which you know God is calling you to go to and speak new life. I pray that you go for it and as you do you begin to see church, not necessarily as you knew it, but church as God wants it to be, really happen.

CHAPTER 9: CAN YOU SEE WHAT IT IS YET?

'No eye has seen, no ear has heard, no mind has conceived what God has prepared for those who love him'

1 CORINTHIANS 2:9 NIV

I was born in 1963 and growing up in the '60s and early '70s life was lived outdoors a lot more than it is now as there was not much on the television and no such things as computers or video games. So my friends and I kept ourselves busy, and as far as I can remember, blissfully happy, with endless games of football in the streets, hide and seek and perhaps a few not quite so wholesome activities around our neighbourhood.

However, I do remember when we got a television for the first time. It was 1970 and Dad had got it for the Mexico World Cup. Scotland hadn't qualified, but Pele was at the peak of his powers and well worth watching and there was always the chance that someone would give reigning world champions England a 'doing'! Thanks to West Germany, this happened and Dad had a very happy summer! I apologise to all my English friends for this confession and freely admit that we Scots can indeed be very petty and small-minded, but at least we're honest about it.

Our first television was black and white and then we moved on to a colour set that was a rental one. It had a slot meter into which we had to insert fifty pence coins in order to watch programmes. When I tell my children this, they think I'm making it up and laugh at how old I am. It was also a time when there were only two channels to watch and programming was restricted to only part of the day before the test card would appear. We now have Sky TV with over 900 channels and 24 hours of endless programmes and the world has changed enormously. Nevertheless, irritatingly I often can't find anything to watch, or I spend ages channel-hopping just in case there's something better on another channel that I wouldn't want to miss!

There was, however, one particular television show that I do remember watching every Saturday night as a young boy – The Rolf Harris Show. It was great, honest! The highlight of the show for me was when Rolf did a live painting on a huge canvas with big brushes, as he jumped around laughing, humming and making strange huffing and puffing noises. For kids today this may seem laughable and almost bizarre for prime time TV on a Saturday night. They have Ant and Dec, 'The X-Factor', 'Britain's Got Talent' and 'Gladiators' and we literally 'watched paint dry' live on television! But this was far from boring, it was fascinating and absorbing television to me and, I am sure, to many of my generation. Rolf would start with a blank canvas and just make what seemed like random brush strokes and for ages it looked a complete mess. Then a picture would appear and as it started to take the form that the artist intended, Rolf would say in his distinctive Aussie accent, 'Can you see what it is yet?'

For kids today this may seem laughable and almost bizarre for prime time TV on a Saturday night.

If I knew, I would scream the answer at the telly, hopefully before any of my family got it and if I couldn't tell what it was, I would get excited knowing that I would soon see. In truth, I was never disappointed by what I saw, as it was always something different from what I had expected at the start and there was a great sense of satisfaction in the end to see the artist's imagination come to life on this canvas before my eyes.

Since then, I have often thought that the church as it should be, is a bit like Rolf's television paintings. It starts blank, with nothing more than the artist's imagination and as it progresses there is no way of guessing what it will end up like. At times it may even look a complete mess, but in the end the artist's vision appears and what comes to view is spectacularly creative and unique. Like Rolf's paintings the church is becoming something and there is a definite plan and picture which will emerge in time, even if it doesn't always look that way. In the end, it will be all the artist ever wanted it to be. But no matter how good any painting Rolf or any other artist has ever done is, it could never compare to what God is making the church into.

On God's eternal canvas and with His holy brush strokes, the church is becoming something that is unlike anything else that has ever been conceived of and it is incomparably more amazing than anything any artist could create. To Jesus, the church is becoming the most beautiful and spectacular creation of all, His bride. That alone is the picture that is being painted on God's canvas and when He has finished and asks heaven if they can see what it is yet, a beautiful, pure bride will be all there is to be seen.

> To Jesus, the church is becoming the most beautiful and spectacular creation of all, His bride.

I have been married to Maggie for twenty five years and I know what it feels like to stand at the altar with a beautiful bride, so in love and so stunned by this woman's beauty inside and out that it almost took my breath away, in partial disbelief at how lucky I was that she would ever want to spend her life with me. Like all ministers and pastors I have had the privilege of standing beside many young men and women as they commit themselves in marriage to one another for the rest of their lives. In particular, I watch the way the man looks at his bride that first time. I know that look.

Of all the things I have seen in my ministry, I am convinced that there is something uniquely passionate about that moment, particularly from a guy's perspective. Looking at the groom's eyes or sensing something of the love and passion expressed in his words and his heart in that moment on his wedding day. I usually encourage the groom to be relaxed and if he wants to turn round and watch her walk down the aisle to just go for it. Don't let tradition or the stiffness of the occasion or his shirt collar get in the way, just look at that girl! It is wonderful to see his face, all the love, all the passion, all the excitement, all the anticipation. 'Wow! She is mine and I get to keep her and love her forever!' Incredible as it may seem, that is exactly how Jesus sees the church and how He will feel one day as we are eternally united with Him.

There are two things I find amazing about this. Firstly, that the creator of the universe could think that way about us; this truly staggers me. What a privilege. But also having been in the church for nearly thirty years and in full-time ministry for twenty five of those, how on earth could Jesus find us so attractive? You may also feel this way. After all there's much about the church that's not all that attractive. In fact there are times when some of the ugliest and most unholy behaviour I have ever seen in life I have seen in the church, including my own. How could Jesus possibly love us when we're like that? How could He possibly prize us so much that He sees us as His beloved, pure bride that He has waited all eternity for, when we can be so horrible, selfish and ungracious? Of all the mysteries of God,

> How could He possibly prize us so much that He sees us as His beloved, pure bride that He has waited all eternity for, when we can be so horrible, selfish and ungracious?

for me that's one of the greatest. Of all the demonstrations of how amazing God's grace really is, it is hard to beat the fact that He longs for the church as a groom longs for his bride.

The secret is though, that Jesus doesn't see us as we began or even as we are now. He sees us for what we will become, when the Spirit's work of sanctification is complete, when the old has passed away and the new has come and when all that is only seen dimly now will be seen clearly then as it actually is. He doesn't just see the blank canvas or the messy brush strokes in the middle. He sees the finished article. He sees how we end up and to Him it is the most beautiful thing created in the entire universe. One day He will watch us walking down heaven's aisle, with His eyes fixed on our every move and His heart beating fast with eternal love and will say, 'Wow! She is mine and I get to keep her and love her forever!'

The church is becoming something. 'Can you see what it is yet?' It is becoming Jesus' bride. You and I are becoming something that Jesus prizes and longs for. So if you are in a place of frustration by what you can see or feel in your own life, in the congregation you belong to or in the church as a whole then be encouraged. It will not always be that way and something beautiful is coming. If the church that you see is not just far from looking like a beautiful bride but at the moment looks more like the bride of Frankenstein, then don't despair. Look again and see what God sees; our potential.

> *You and I are becoming something that Jesus prizes and longs for.*

Then, once you've looked, seek His heart on what we will become and what we can do to help us get there, because we have to do our part too. The bride doesn't get down the aisle looking like she does by accident! There are months, sometimes years of preparation and attention to detail, care and hard work. She does her utmost to let her husband see her at her best at that moment. She doesn't turn up in her jeans or joggers with morning hair and no make-up. She honours him, and herself, by the effort she makes for her husband at that moment and for the start of the life they will share together. The one thing she can't do is make him love her, but he's already made that choice. This is just a public confirmation of that fact.

Similarly, we don't have to work to make Jesus love us or long for us, since He already does that. But what we do have to know is that there is a wedding date set and there is a time coming when we will be joining Him at the altar and so we must be absolutely determined that we will do all we can to be as beautifully prepared and ready for that moment as we can be.

To my mind, what makes the church its most beautiful and the way in which we can prepare ourselves to be ready to stand as that longed-for bride at the altar with Christ, is to live out the Great Commandments – to love God with all our heart, soul, mind and strength and to love our neighbour as ourselves. These two commandments don't just change us, they change the world around us, for they make us what God wants us to be. Jesus put such emphasis on them that He said if we get these two things right, all the rest will take care of itself.

> *These two commandments don't just change us, they change the world around us, for they make us what God wants us to be.*

Two words describe the outworking of these two greatest commandments: passion and compassion. Passion for God, for His name, His presence, His honour and His glory, expressed in worship that seeks Him in Spirit and truth, worship that is desperate for Him and Him alone and lives that can never be complete without Him. This is the spring of living water that bubbles up within us as we long to know and worship a holy God. Then the overflow of this worship and the practical outworking of this is when the church lives the kind of lives that reflect this heart towards our Father and reflect His heart towards our neighbour.

Passion without compassion won't work, since at best it can only give us a zealous 'religion' which the world needs more of as much as it needs another hole in the ozone layer. Neither is compassion on its own enough, because it won't be driven from a heart after God and will only give part of what the world really needs. It would be to try to have the second great commandment without the first. One is the heart and the other the life-blood that flows from it. True compassion begins when we connect with God and reach out from there with compassion for the lost, the poor and the broken. We have to be passionate with compassion for God's justice and mercy.

As I look at the church in our land and around the world, those churches that are making a real difference to their community always have those two features prominent in their life and witness and nothing makes them more attractive or effective. I have great respect and admiration for the ministry of Hillsong Church in Sydney, Australia and for its Senior Pastors Brian and Bobbie Houston and Worship Pastor Darlene Zschech. This church, I believe, has 'got it'. I particularly like the way they explain their vision statement. They call it 'The Church That I See'[xiv] and in it they outline all that the church is and is becoming from what to me, looks like God's heart perspective for them as Christ's bride.

It is a statement of intent and purpose declaring all that the church was meant to be, is becoming and will become in its response to God as creator and Father, Jesus as Saviour and Lord and by the Holy Spirit as God's power working in the church to change us and the world around us. Theirs is a vision of a beautiful and attractive church. One that is not only winsome to Jesus but to the watching world around it. Having been there, I believe they are indeed reaching for this vision with such Godly intent that they really are seeing the church that God sees. No, it is not the perfect church, nor is it the only good one around the world and I'm sure there will be things they could do better, but I believe they are right to emphasise who they can be and who they are becoming.

> *Theirs is a vision of a beautiful and attractive church. One that is not only winsome to Jesus but to the watching world around it.*

There are many churches that could learn from this as we seek to be all we can be and perhaps pay more attention to our appearance and attractiveness in and to Jesus both inside and out. This in itself will make us more attractive to the world and will draw people to us and what we are about. Another amazing fact about a bride on her wedding day is that everyone else at the wedding agrees with her husband that she is indeed beautiful! If we become

---

xiv 'The Church That I See' can be read in full on www.hillsong.com

all that Jesus longs for us to be the watching world will agree with him, don't you worry about that!

Of course, we cannot make the church what it will become on our own and no amount of good intent or hard work in itself will get us there. Like all successful marriages it is a partnership, it is a combination of grace, of a sovereign work of God's Spirit working in us with our obedient co-operation. We cannot make God come and move in a place, but we can work with Him and do the things He asks of us. We cannot make the wind of the Spirit blow, but we can trim and set our sails in preparation for when He does. In so doing we will become as He envisioned us to be. God alone is the artist; the church was His idea; He conceived it in His imagination and He will ultimately make it appear as He intends it to be – that awesomely beautiful bride of Christ. When He's finished, heaven will gasp and Jesus will love it! The church is becoming something. 'Can you see what it is yet?'

CHAPTER 10: YO ADRIAN WE DID IT!

"'It is not by might nor by power, but by my Spirit says the Lord.'"

ZECHARIAH 4:6 NIV

Movies can do much more than just entertain us. Like all forms of mass media, they have the power to influence individuals and society as a whole for good and for evil. Yet at their best they can challenge or reinforce our values, cause us to see things in a wonderful new way and inspire us and help us to reach for the stars! Is that not why Hollywood remains so popular and has such a huge influence on society and why so much money is spent on its perpetuation? In recent years I have had a fascination with finding signs of God and His Kingdom in the movies. This really started to interest me when I was studying for my M.Th. in The Theology & Ethics of Communication at New College in 1996-97 and in particular as I wrote a Masters dissertation on theological motifs in Hollywood films. Although I was looking at a number of mainstream movies at the time, my main case study was Mel Gibson's epic, 'Braveheart'[xv] and I wrote a paper called *'Braveheart: a Salvation Story'* which to my surprise was chosen for publication in a theological journal, although I suspect it was only ever bought by a dozen people!

I have also always loved the 'Rocky' movies. Since Rocky Balboa, nicknamed 'The Italian Stallion', first appeared on the big screens in 1976 in the ultimate David and Goliath story, this character, portrayed now in six films by Sylvester Stallone, has touched and inspired me and a good few of the big inspirational lines from the

---

xv   Braveheart, Directed by Mel Gibson, Icon Productions, Twentieth Century Fox, 1995

Rocky movies have featured in sermons and talks I've done over the years. I know some may laugh at this and see these as films for the Neanderthal man and my love of them as me reverting to this type, but I don't care, Rocky has never let me down (apart from some parts of 'Rocky V', which were a bit dodgy!) and I am proud to say he has given me much needed motivation and inspiration in my life and ministry on many an occasion. Whenever I hear the Rocky soundtrack, recently voted the most inspirational music by the world's sportspeople, it does something to me.

But Rocky is not just a film about boxing, it is a love story between Rocky and his beloved wife Adrian. It charts the way they come together, fight the world together and love and support one another through thick and thin. No-one who has seen the movies could fail to be moved when Rocky finally wins the World Heavyweight Championship belt, despite taking an incredible amount of physical punishment, as he grabs the announcer's microphone and shouts, 'Yo Adrian we did it'. A testimony to how much they did it together. Fittingly, it is also the last line spoken in 'Rocky Balboa', the sixth and probably final instalment of the series, in which Adrian is now dead, as he visits her grave after his ultimate fight.

Rocky's story is also a story about overcoming the odds, training and fighting to be all that we can be and never giving up on our dreams, all of which are for me absolutely sound Biblical principles. Interestingly, in the movies Rocky is always seen praying before a big fight and going to church in times of real trial. In the last movie, a minor character from the first film, a former opponent called Spider Rico, re-appears as a real friend in Rocky's life. Spider is a Christian and on the evening of Rocky's big fight against the much younger current world champion, whilst in the dressing room before the fight, he reads these words from Zechariah to Rocky, "'It is not by might nor by power, but by my Spirit says the Lord.'" (Zechariah 4:6 NIV).

Rocky was always the underdog and he was often against the ropes, almost out on his feet and ready for the final blow to finish him off. On many occasions he was written off as finished, washed up and told he should give up because no-one believed in him any more. Despite all that, he always believed in himself and he never gave up! I think the quotation from Zechariah is an interesting one in many ways, for by this point in his career if Rocky has anything he has might and power in abundance. I think this is hilariously highlighted when his trainer, Duke, comments that he will hit his opponent so hard that 'his ancestors will feel it'.

> One thing will get him through this fight, the Spirit of the Lord.

But even with all this natural and physically honed might and power, Rocky is reminded that it is not enough, only one thing will get him through this fight, the Spirit of the Lord. At this Rocky gets on his knees once again and the viewer is left concluding that it is indeed this which he seeks in his hour of greatest need.

In this book so far, I've compared the church as it is in Scotland today to an army, a pile of bones, an eagle, something from Star Trek, a Rolf Harris painting and a bride, some of which you may just about have bought, but comparing it to Rocky?, 'Come on Jim, you're taking this a bit far!' I hear you say. Well bear with me, for I think we have some things we can learn from 'The Italian Stallion' and his story.

The first obvious comparison is that for some, the church is nearing the end of the line as quickly as Rocky at the end of his career and is very much on the ropes. Humanism, individualism, pluralism, secularism and all the other 'isms' Scotland has embraced are supposedly pounding the life out of us and we're about to hit the canvas and won't get back up for the count of ten. Then there's the fact that some of the things we once prized are gone, like his Adrian, dead and buried. Ways of working and things once cherished are no longer alive in this land. Add to this the ageing profile and creaking bones in the pews and the once mighty and powerful Church in Scotland appears to many to be just like Rocky at the end of his career, a bit past it in the face of younger, fitter opponents. Any might and power the church once had is not enough to turn this around and win this fight. So what do we have left? That's right, just like good old Rocky was reminded by his friend Spider Rico before his last contest, all we have left is indeed 'the Spirit of the Lord!' Well wow! What a weapon to have in our corner!

Praise God if getting to this point in history has led us to realise this and stop mourning the days gone by and weapons we used to have and don't any more and has caused us to start using the most amazing one of all which we still do have. The Spirit of the Lord God Almighty lives in us. The power that raised Jesus from the dead is within us and it is at our disposal. All the authority and all the power we can ever need to access everything that God's Kingdom here on earth has for us is ours by right, because Jesus said so. We have the

> *The Spirit of the Lord God Almighty lives in us. The power that raised Jesus from the dead is within us and it is at our disposal.*

collective energy, creativity and will of heaven placed in us to do the works Jesus left us to do. So much so, that Jesus said we'd do the things He did and even more than He did because of this deposit of heaven in us and therefore His going back to the Father was not to our detriment but to our gain! I think most of us neither understand this nor tap into it, yet we still plod on trying to do God's work here on earth without it. I know I did for a long time in my ministry and I ended up on the same ropes that so many burnt out ministers, pastors and church leaders have fallen back on to before me.

When I initially arrived at my first charge as minister of Oldmachar I had no clue as to how I might build this new church plant from where it was to the place where I felt God wanted it to be and where I knew it needed to be to become a Kingdom influence on the community, city and hopefully on the nation. After trying really hard for a while and seeing some things happen, but nothing like I had hoped for and being a bit punch-drunk in the process, I was in prayer one day, crying out to God for help and I felt Him say, 'You've tried *your* ministry and you've seen the results. What about trying *my* ministry now?' This was to change my life and my idea of what my calling and ministry were, as I let go and let God do His stuff. I soon discovered that His ministry is far better than mine! No matter how good your ministry is, I respectfully suggest that His might be better than yours too. So, if you're struggling to see anything happen in your ministry and feel like giving up, can I suggest you do just that? Give up *your* ministry and allow God to do His. It will blow your mind and abundantly more than all you had hoped and dreamed of will start to happen.

> *The turning point for me was total surrender to the Spirit of the Lord Almighty and laying aside all my perceived 'might and power'.*

The turning point for me was total surrender to the Spirit of the Lord Almighty and laying aside all my perceived 'might and power', all the things I thought I could do in my strength and with my gifts. I'm not saying our gifts and our effort are not required, what I am saying is that on their own they are not enough! To win this fight, it is not going to happen by might nor by power but by the Spirit of the Lord.

I know for some reading this, the very mention of the Spirit's work will cause them to throw up their guard and will lead to suspicion and I can understand that. The Holy Spirit has had such a bad press and a raw deal in the church and as a result, on the whole, I see most of the church with a lopsided Trinity where at one extreme the Holy Spirit is the Holy-Everything and at the other he is the Holy-Nothing. What we need is a balanced view of the Spirit's person, His work in our lives and in the church and the world.

Some in the church emphasise the gifts of the Spirit as the be all and end all, whilst others who reject the gifts as ours for today, simply accentuate the fruit. But surely they cannot be separated. Indeed, if they are, I believe it can be disastrous.

I come from a place in the theological landscape that some would call 'charismatic' and although labels are not always helpful, I am fairly comfortable with that. Yet I have to say that I have witnessed some of the most unbalanced expressions of the Spirit's work in some places within that which would call itself the charismatic church, where the gifts of the Spirit have been exercised without the fruit of the Spirit. Without love, patience and self-control, the gifts of the Spirit can be clumsy, insensitive and simply convince the world that we are all crazy. It can have the effect of a firework being set off in someone's clenched fist, resulting in people being hurt. The gifts of the Spirit, without the fruit of the Spirit are no good. God is One and He is not able to be compartmentalised. The revelation He gives us of Himself in Scripture is holistic.

> Without love, patience and self-control, the gifts of the Spirit can be clumsy, insensitive and simply convince the world that we are all crazy.

Accordingly, the fruit of the Spirit without the gifts, is also no good and a distortion of the Biblical revelation of who God is and how He works in His church and in the world. To try to be the church today without the gifts of the Spirit operating in the church, will both deny the church the tools it needs to do the job and will cut off the power supply required to get it done. As I write this chapter the road outside our house is being dug up to fit new drains and manhole covers. The workmen have a huge digger and a pneumatic drill to break the tarmac and make the hole they need to do their job. They came 'tooled up' for the job and thankfully they didn't come with a garden shovel or a teaspoon. It may have been possible eventually to dig a hole with either of these, but we wouldn't have been getting our nice hole-free road back very quickly.

Others may argue with this from their own experience, but I really could not have made any impact in the community God called me to minister in and I could not have built a church without the present reality of the whole work of the Spirit of the Lord.

Whenever I tried, it was like digging into granite with a teaspoon. Yet when I allowed the Spirit to be in control, His ministry was like the pneumatic drill that was needed to break the ground and make some Kingdom progress. So my view of my role changed, I was no longer *the* minister, *the* Senior Pastor, *the* evangelist, *the* worship leader or *the* key leader of the church. The Holy Spirit was and I was working with Him in the role and within the gifting He had given me, but He was always in charge. Before I ever stood to lead God's people in worship, I always invited the Holy Spirit to come and be the worship leader. Nothing gets you deeper into the presence of God than when God's Spirit is leading you there. Whenever we prayed I would ask the Holy Spirit to allow His prayers and groans which were already deep within us to come out as God's heart cry from within. This revolutionised my prayer life and that of our corporate prayer.

People have often asked me questions like, 'How can I pray in God's will?' or, 'Is it right to pray for healing in this situation?' or, 'How do I know God's will and call in my life?' Initially those questions had me in all sorts of theological contortions trying to find something that would satisfy both our free-will and God's sovereignty. But now I've taken the pressure off me and the people who ask this, by simply pointing to the fact that if we allow Him, God's Spirit is already praying within us and so if we really want to know what God wants us to pray, why don't we let God within us pray through us? We just need to let these prayers well up and burst out. This is not a cop-out from us expressing our own heart cries and deep desires and leaving it all to God, for in my experience, it is when we allow the Spirit to groan through our prayers, that our heart actually connects with God and what we really want to say in prayer comes out.

> We just need to let these prayers well up and burst out.

I think it's the same with preaching. All our wise words and compelling arguments without the dynamic of the Spirit flowing through them are just more words. I heard someone say on television last night, 'A man with an experience outranks a man with an argument'. I think this is true. An experience gives us a testimony and it is our testimony which changes us. In Revelation it says the believers overcame Satan by, *'the blood of the Lamb and the word of their testimony'* (Revelation 12:11 NIV). When I preach, I don't want people to be convinced by my arguments or impressed by the articulation of my words, I want them to experience God and for that experience to be life-changing and form the testimony by which they overcome.

I studied for nine years and have three theological degrees and I am clearly not at all against theological study, hermeneutical discipline or homiletical training and excellence. I think we need great preachers in the church who have studied hard and who work hard to communicate the Gospel really well, but I maintain that this in and of itself will not be enough, certainly not any more in this world of endless words and multiple means of communication, most of which are not just talking heads.

Our words will not change people, but the Spirit's voice through our words. When God communicates to people, as we can see from all of Scripture and all the historical accounts we have of how God speaks to men and women, it is not a one-dimensional communication involving the brain alone. God is not stuck in the cerebral, linear communication that much of the church is. He speaks in 3-D, multi-sensory, holistic ways and this is what ultimately changes lives. So whenever I speak or preach now I am not interested in just my words coming out, I want the Spirit of the Lord to speak through me.

Whenever I speak or preach now I am not interested in just my words coming out, I want the Spirit of the Lord to speak through me.

I want Him to be the preacher and always invite Him to be so. Like most preachers, I tend to think I am quite good at it, but as I said above, He's better. My words can at best change people's mind, His words through me can change their eternal destiny.

This principle also works in evangelism, teaching, vision, strategy, compassion, pastoral care and every other aspect of the church's ministry. Let the Spirit's power be the only driving force behind what we do. That way we will always know the right direction and always know the how, when and why of our ministry. Now add our personal gifts, effort and drive to that and we will really begin to go somewhere! In all of this I believe we start to discover the secret of building a church and a community of faith that affects a change and can re-shape and re-define the world around it. We will see the impact of stopping relying on our own might and power and begin to fully rely on Spirit of the Lord. The landscape around us will change and we will see visible signposts that this change is happening.

> Let the Spirit's power be the only driving force behind what we do.

There were a few great landmarks in our ministry in Oldmachar and signposts of where we were heading started to appear. At the moment of each, I had a great sense of satisfaction that something good for the Kingdom had been achieved and we were going where God was leading us. One example of this is when we started to see a real change of atmosphere in our worship as we learnt how to go deeper with God and people began to come and be transformed in His presence. Another is when we had fifty days of prayer, morning and night, and a new holiness and sense of reverence before God grew amongst us. Also, whenever people were healed and set free from addiction and compulsive behaviour as the Kingdom of God broke out around us. Significantly, when our community started to notice we were there and came to know Jesus was for them, hundreds returned prayer cards to us asking for God's power and help in their lives. Also when we began to reach out in compassion to hurting people in Vietnam, Ukraine, Kenya, India and to the people in our own city and nation and when we saw that our money could talk and speak the language of the Kingdom as we sowed it generously. Then when young people who had come to faith in Jesus and had grown through the church's discipleship and mentoring became leaders in key areas of worship and ministry in the congregation as gifting and attitude, not age, were the main qualifications.

Again, when we saw a real breakthrough in our schools ministry as we reached out to tens of thousands of young people in Jesus' name in a contemporary way and the schools asked us to come to them. When the vision for *The One Band* was born to further develop this and when our ministry team that had begun with just me, had grown to twelve full-time and part-time members. At the time when the church became the first New Charge Development congregation ever to move to Full Status within the Church of Scotland and we were able to share something of God's faithfulness in this to the national church as a whole at the General Assembly in 2007. And finally when God called Maggie and me to The Scotland Trust and the people in Oldmachar knew this was of God and sent us out with love and joy that the Kingdom was advancing.

> *'We did it! Not by might, nor by power but by the Spirit of the Lord'.*

On each occasion as we saw what God was doing Maggie and I could say, 'We did it! Not by might, nor by power but by the Spirit of the Lord'.

CHAPTER 11: DESPERATE!

'From the days of John the Baptist until now, the kingdom of heaven has been forcefully advancing and forceful men lay hold of it'

MATTHEW 11:12 NIV

Over the last few years one of the most popular television programmes imported from the States has been 'Desperate Housewives'. My two oldest daughters Pam and Dawn and my wife Maggie have, at various times, been hooked on the show so in the interests of family harmony when they have been watching it, I have not tried to grab the remote control and switch over to the football as I would have preferred, but I have watched it with them. I can say without doubt that watching 'Desperate Housewives' has not really changed my life, but it has got me some brownie points from the girls for sitting through it with them!

However, it has made me think about what it means to be desperate. Perhaps we should make a TV show called, 'Desperate Christians' or 'Desperate Churches'. I have often thought that much of the church has been desperate, but not in a good way! I think some of our attempts to communicate our faith, as well as who we are and what we are about, have been so poor that one would have to be desperate to want to go there on a regular basis.

> *Perhaps we should make a TV show called, 'Desperate Christians' or 'Desperate Churches'.*

Yet there is a kind of desperation that I think is good and am sure we should all have it as followers of Jesus; desperation to know Him more and to do the things He did. We should be desperate to become like Him and to be consumed by Him; desperate for His presence and His glory, for His Kingdom to come and His will to be done on earth as it is in heaven[xvi]. That kind of desperation changes us, it does not allow us to settle for mediocrity and it drives us on to greater things. That kind of desperation causes us to do some damage to the kingdom of darkness.

> We should be desperate to become like Him and to be consumed by Him; desperate for His presence and His glory, for His Kingdom to come and His will to be done on earth as it is in heaven

I have always greatly admired Billy Graham for his willingness to go to the ends of the earth to preach the Gospel to millions with such obvious love for the Lord and for the lost. Equally the ministry of Oral Roberts, who probably personally prayed for and laid hands on more people than anyone else in history, was one of such desperate love for Jesus and the sick people he prayed for. I also love the way evangelist Reinhard Bonke explains his ministry, which is seeing millions of people across the world, especially in Africa, find liberation in Jesus, as 'Plundering hell and populating heaven'. These are forceful words from a forceful man, yet they are also Kingdom words; words that only come from a heart that is desperate for the lost and really does see their plight as hopeless without Jesus. Of course it is one thing to recognise this, but it is quite another to do something about it.

Over the years I have been convinced that as a church we have often been trying so hard to be nice and to be liked by everyone, for fear that we might offend anyone, that we have become too safe and have lost our cutting edge for mission. We have not exactly been storming the gates of hell, laying hold of the Kingdom and forcefully advancing it as Jesus suggests we might. Do not get me wrong, there is nothing bad about being nice and we all like to be liked. I am also

xvi   See Matthew 6:10

not advocating that we are offensive in the way we minister.

Nonetheless, we do need to remember that, as Paul says, we are in a spiritual battle. It is one in which we are expected to fight and as we do so we will get our hands dirty. Paul explains it like this; '*This is no afternoon athletic contest that we'll walk away from and forget about in a couple of hours. This is for keeps, a life-or-death fight to the finish against the Devil and all his angels*'. (Ephesians 6:12 TM)

At many points in our ministry at Oldmachar Church and in the first few months of this new ministry adventure in The Scotland Trust, whenever we have been making ground and what I would call Kingdom progress, we have been subject to a ferocious backlash of opposition, criticism, financial hardship and, at times, ill-health.

All of these things that we have gone through are clearly physical, human experiences, but in my mind they all have a very real spiritual origin. It seems crazy to say after having been in full-time ministry for 25 years, but when this happens it sometimes takes me by surprise and I go running off to God to ask Him why things are so tough. He usually reminds me of two things; firstly, that He loves me and is with me and secondly, that this is all part of what it means to take up my cross and follow Jesus and that to go and make disciples in His name does not come cheap! Yet what should we expect? If we do make Kingdom progress in our ministries, do we honestly think the devil is going to pat us on the back and send us a congratulatory telegram? Of course not! He and all the powers of darkness are going to resist every attempt we make to push them backwards, bring light into the darkness and set the captives free.

One of my favourite books in recent years has been 'The Barbarian Way' by Erwin McManus [xvii] in which he speaks of the pioneering Christians who drive back the darkness and take ground for the Kingdom of God as being like the early Barbarians who

xvii   Erwin McManus, The Barbarian Way, Nelson Books, 2005

were almost unstoppable and untameable in their zeal to win new lands and territory. McManus hints that, as a church, we have become too civilised and suggests that it is time for some Barbarian spirit to emerge amongst God's people today. I certainly resonate with this and was excited to read his book since it helped me understand myself better as well as some of the frustration I feel at the tremendous amount of time and energy we tend to waste on doing things that in the end mean nothing, achieve nothing and amount to nothing.

I am convinced that it is time, in our land, for us to be a bit more forceful and purposeful in our vision and that we must start to take more seriously the battle we are in for the heart and soul of our nation. None of this cuts across grace, nor does it conflict with the fruit of the Spirit in us, for as always, our weapons are love, joy, peace, mercy and justice where the people we are trying to reach in Jesus' name are concerned. Our battle, as Paul reminds us, is not with flesh and blood[xviii]. We are not to fight with flesh and blood we are to love it in Jesus' name!

> *I am convinced that it is time, in our land, for us to be a bit more forceful and purposeful in our vision and that we must start to take more seriously the battle we are in for the heart and soul of our nation.*

However, we are not to make any allowances or take any prisoners with the enemy we wrestle with, as he is the thief of all that is good and his only agenda is, as Jesus put it, *'To steal, kill and destroy'* (John 10:10 NIV). We want to offer people the life in all its fullness that Jesus gives, but we do have to deal with the thief first. Or, as Jesus put it elsewhere, if we want to rob the strong man we have to *'tie him up first'*. [xix] The implication here is that if you do not recognise with whom you are dealing and deal with him properly, you will be in trouble and will get a bloody nose.

---

xviii See Ephesians 6:12

xix   See Matthew 12:29

Perhaps as Christians it is time that we took seriously the fact that we have an adversary who has amassed a huge force of evil against us, the church. This is a force whose weapons of destruction are aimed directly at us with the sole purpose of stealing all that is good and of God in our lives; of destroying our name, our reputation, our ministries and our finances and of actually killing us and the life of God in us. This is not the cute little devil with the tail and toasting fork that we see in 'Tom and Jerry' cartoons. This is the roaring lion that Peter warns is a very real enemy, who is on the prowl seeking to *'devour us'*. (1 Peter 5:8 NIV)

In order to make ground in the face of such real opposition Jesus seems to be suggesting that we need to be desperate people and just as forceful and purposeful in our mission as our adversary is in his. And here's the best part, we have the weapons at our disposal in and through the name of Jesus, that guarantee we will win. In order to do so, we have to take them up and we have to fight. In this fight the weapons we have are the name and the authority of Jesus. These are the secrets to the Kingdom of God and seeing its fruit manifest before our eyes in the lives of individuals, in whole communities, cities and nations. In recent days I have been praying and thinking more about the Kingdom of God than almost anything else, because I see this as being the key to the church's mission and to the restoration of the name and the glory of Jesus that I and so many others long to see in our nation.

Jesus was the ultimate Kingdom man; in fact He actually was the Kingdom of God in the flesh.

Jesus was the ultimate Kingdom man; in fact He actually was the Kingdom of God in the flesh. Wherever He went and whatever He did, He did it with a Kingdom agenda in obedience to His Father, the King! This is how the start of His ministry is explained in Mark's Gospel, *'Jesus preached the gospel of the Kingdom of God saying, "The time is fulfilled, the Kingdom of God is at hand. Repent and believe"'*. (Mark 1:14-15 NIV)

How this was outworked in Jesus' ministry amongst real people is also described in Mark; *'He healed the sick and cast out many demons'.* (Mark 1:34 NIV) As a result of this, wherever He went, His Kingdom displaced the kingdom of darkness. John explains that this should not come as a surprise to us, because it is actually the very reason He was incarnated; *'For this purpose the Son of God was manifested, that he might destroy the works of the devil'* (1 John 3:8 NKJV). The Kingdom of God is at the heart of the ministry of Jesus, the testimony of the Gospels and the Epistles, the call and commission of the church and the consummation of all things at the end of time, (see Revelation). We are expected to be Kingdom people like the One we follow.

However, it is important to know that the Kingdom of God is not a matter of words only but of power. From that power come visible signs that the Kingdom is among us, just like it did when Jesus walked the earth. The visible signs of the Kingdom in Jesus' ministry were plain for all to witness: the blind could see, the lame could walk and the dead were raised. Jesus' Kingdom ministry visibly changed things and I am convinced that ours should too, for the Kingdom of God is within us. The same Spirit that raised Jesus from the dead lives in us and

> *Jesus' Kingdom ministry visibly changed things and I am convinced that ours should too, for the Kingdom of God is within us.*

because of this, Jesus Himself anticipated that we would do all the things He did; in fact He actually said we would do even greater things than He did [xx].

To my mind this is the crux of the matter for the church today, as we seek to reclaim the territory we have lost over generations in our land. Where are the visible signs of the Kingdom amongst us? If all that Jesus said is true, they should be there. For not only is the Kingdom within us, because of this it is expected to come out of us!

---

xx   See John 14:12

We are meant to be infectious Kingdom-carriers and Kingdom-spreaders. I will never forget travelling to Toronto in 2003 when the world was panicking about the outbreak of the SARS virus. SARS, or severe acute respiratory syndrome, is a respiratory disease in humans which is highly contagious and can be deadly. Between November 2002 and July 2003 there was a lot of talk of a near pandemic, with 8,096 known infected cases and 774 deaths worldwide being listed in the World Health Organization's (WHO) April 21, 2004 concluding report of what happened during that time. One of the cities in the world affected by the SARS outbreak was Toronto and flying in and out of the airport there was unnerving as all the airport staff were wearing masks to stop them from catching and spreading the virus. This was not a pleasant place to be at that time, but everyone was aware of the infectiousness of this virus and the authorities were doing all they could to prevent it being spread.

> *We should make such an impact wherever we go that our presence there is visible for all to see and the lives we touch will forever be changed for coming into contact with us.*

The church of Jesus Christ should be as infectious as that, but not infectious with sickness and death, the opposite in fact; infectious with the life of Jesus! We should make such an impact wherever we go that our presence there is visible for all to see and the lives we touch will forever be changed for coming into contact with us.

We should be the sort of people that the 'authorities' of hell consider dangerous to come into their region. Light and life should accompany our ministry and darkness and death should be expelled wherever we go. Why, then, is this so rarely the case? Could it be that we are not desperate enough for the Kingdom? Is it perhaps that we are not forceful enough as Kingdom people? Do we need to lay hold of the Kingdom more and cause it to advance wherever we are and wherever we go?

Over the last month or so I have been witnessing the effects of the ministry of a very forceful and truly desperate man, the Canadian evangelist, Todd Bentley. Since early April 2008, Todd has been leading nightly meetings in Lakeland, Florida in what has become known by some as the 'Lakeland Revival' and by others as the 'Florida Outpouring'. Hundreds of thousands of people have been attending his healing meetings and millions around the world have been watching events from Lakeland on GOD TV and on the internet. Todd Bentley originally went to conduct a series of four meetings at a church in Lakeland, but such was the impact of the ministry and the outpouring of the Spirit people sensed there, that the meetings kept going and the venues kept growing. As they did, so did the tens of thousands of testimonies of miraculous healings and even reports of over a dozen resurrections!

Such was the impact of the ministry and the outpouring of the Spirit people sensed there, that the meetings kept going and the venues kept growing.

As always with these things the church was almost immediately split by the events in Lakeland. Many embraced the outpouring as a move of God that would have global impact and thousands flew to Florida for an 'impartation'; to receive a bit of the tangible presence of God and the fire they felt was falling there, to take it home to their church, community, city and nation. From this there have been reports of similar outbreaks of healings and miracles all over the world by people who went to Lakeland. Along with this, as one would expect, there have been many in the church who have rejected this because they have seen it as a move of the devil, a large-scale deception or the work of a false prophet. Some have been truly offended by the unconventional style and methods of Todd who, when he prays for people, lays hands on them and as a sort of signal that the Spirit is about to come upon them he says 'Bam!' as he speaks healing in Jesus' name. Not your average Sunday morning church service by any means!

However, Todd is not your average minister and certainly does not fit with the stereotypical image of a North American TV evangelist. He doesn't have 'the $500 suit', as he puts it and looks like a guy you would be more used to seeing in a bikers' bar. He is tattooed from head to toe and has numerous ear and face piercings. I must confess that the first time I saw him I was immediately struck by how refreshingly different he was and I liked his style!

However, much more than just his appearance is instantly visible, so is his heart and this is a heart that is truly desperate for God and for His presence. As well as this, I was struck by the way he and his ministry took the Kingdom of God by force and how he really did seek a visible demonstration of that Kingdom in the lives of those whom he was praying for.

Such was my interest in what was happening in Lakeland that I started watching the GOD TV broadcast almost every night. I was fascinated because this was not a 'religious' broadcast, this was what appeared to be the Kingdom of God breaking into people's lives live on TV. The stories people shared of what God had done in their lives were stories of the blind seeing, the lame walking, the dead rising and demons being cast out. As I watched the meetings on GOD TV, I thought, "This is clearly going to get some lively debate going in the church and some people are not going to be happy!" But I also thought, "If this *is* of God then the Kingdom is advancing and the devil is not going to be happy". This thought made me *very* happy!

> "If this is of God then the Kingdom is advancing and the devil is not going to be happy".

In my own deliberations, whenever I see or hear of a new 'phenomenon' on the church landscape I usually take a Gamaliel approach[xxi]. If something is not of God then it will not last and God Himself will shut it down, but if it is of God then I do not want to

---

xxi   See Acts 5:22-42

be fighting against it because I would be fighting against Him and that is a fight I would not win. In addition, if it is possible, I will not make a value judgement on hearsay and try to see something for myself before I comment. Incredibly, as this is happening over 3,000 miles away, by God's grace, a few of The Scotland Trust and I were able to go to Lakeland to see for ourselves just what was going on.

On Saturday 3rd May I had been leading worship at the main Saturday night worship celebration of the Church Without Walls National Gathering at Ingliston in Edinburgh. It was a historic weekend overall and this was a fantastic night when God had moved amongst us in great power. There were thousands of

This was a fantastic night when God had moved amongst us in great power.

people packed into the Highland Hall and the Spirit of God was very present. At one point I looked out over the hall to see thousands of people, Church of Scotland members, worshipping Jesus with joyful abandon with smiles on their faces and hands in the air. It was a sight I honestly never thought I would see in such a large way in my own denomination, but one I will also never forget.

After the meeting had finished a few of The Scotland Trust team who had been present at the National Gathering and myself were talking and we were speaking about what we saw happening in Florida and about the possibility of us all going to Lakeland. Over the weekend those of us there and a few who couldn't manage to go to the National Gathering talked and prayed this over and we all felt it was the right thing to go. God provided all we needed financially and practically for this trip, so the following Tuesday five of us flew to Florida for a short four-day visit to the 'Florida Outpouring' and attended three of the meetings.

As I have argued earlier in this book, my theology and experience tell me that God is working everywhere and that His Spirit's fire cannot be contained in one place, I am also not a 'revival tourist' and would not go anywhere *just* for an experience or for the latest Christian fad.

I believe this is also the heart of all of those of who went with me; we are all desperate for God and equally desperate that we see Him move in Kingdom power in our land. We want more than a one-off experience; we want to see the fruit of any move of God's Spirit in the form of changed lives and changed communities in the places to which God has called us. God knows we need to see salvation, miracles, healings and Kingdom outbreaks in Scotland today.

My kids had also been watching the meetings on GOD TV and without our church baggage they had thought they were great and loved Todd's style. My youngest daughter Becky, who is 12 years old and loves Jesus, got really hooked watching the outpouring on TV and would often cry as she saw people, particularly children being healed in Jesus' name. When we were in Lakeland Becky kept texting me to ask how it was going and what God was doing and she would say, 'Have you been 'Bammed' yet?'

> *The time there served to cement the burden and love we have for Scotland.*

Being together in Florida was a great experience and gave us some real time out of our own country to seek God together and pray for our country and this new ministry God has put on our hearts. The time there served to cement the burden and love we have for Scotland.

I do not understand everything Todd does and I would not do everything just like he does, as I am not him, yet his style certainly does not offend me. I would not pray for people with a shout of 'Bam!' as I laid hands on them. Yet I am fascinated by the way he really does go for God and His Kingdom with such forceful ferocity that I believe the God of the Kingdom honours this and gives His visible Kingdom signs in his ministry. I have also been impressed by the obvious fruit his ministry is producing in the name of Jesus and for what always appears to me, for the glory and honour of that name. A clear indicator of whether something is of God or not is the quality and quantity of the fruit it produces. Todd's ministry is producing a huge quantity of fruit and time will tell of the ultimate quality of it, but for now it looks like good fruit to me. The blind are seeing, the lame walking and it even appears that the dead are rising.

We came home from Florida encouraged in two main ways. Firstly, that we had watched God do wonderful things in people's lives as the Kingdom broke through in healing for them. This is always encouraging to see wherever it happens. What Christian would not want to see people being healed? We were also truly encouraged because we knew that we had not witnessed anything we were not now starting to see in our own lives and ministries here in Scotland – in the islands

What Christian would not want to see people being healed?

and mainland of this country God has called us to, if on a smaller scale. These are indeed beginning to be new Kingdom days all over the world as God does pour out His Spirit with fresh fire on His church and the people to whom they are reaching out in His name.

These are also days for brave hearts and forceful men and women who take God at His word and take His Kingdom power, signs and wonders seriously. These are the people who will take the Kingdom of Heaven with them wherever they go. I want to be one of them.

CHAPTER 12: BRINGING DOWN THE GIANTS

"How can we go up? We're trapped in a dead end. Our brothers took all the wind out of our sails, telling us, 'The people are bigger and stronger than we are; their cities are huge, their defenses massive – we even saw Anakite giants there!' "

DEUTERONOMY 1:28 TM

There are moments in the lives of all of us which are life-defining and destiny shaping for us and our God given calling.

In Deuteronomy 1 we see such a moment for Moses and the people of Israel. This story of God's people is fully recorded in Numbers 13 and 14 and makes really interesting reading for any in the church today who are contemplating 'crossing over' into something new. It is especially interesting for Maggie and I and our partners in The Scotland Trust as we stand on the edge of this new moment in our ministry.

It is a time when, after being freed from the oppression of Pharaoh, led out of Egypt, taken across the Red Sea and through a dangerous and desolate desert, the Israelites were standing on the very verge of the Promised Land. In all this time God had led them, protected them and provided for them by His miraculous power and faithfulness. They were now being asked to trust Him one last time and to go and take the land He had promised they would inherit. They were on its border and God said it was all theirs for the taking. This should have been a joyous moment, full of anticipation and excitement.

However, there was a problem! Moses had sent 12 spies into the land to check out the area, the soil, the food and its inhabitants and a majority report had come back that was not a good one. For although the promised land was everything God had said it would be; *'flowing with milk and honey'* (Numbers 13:27 NIV), ten out of the twelve spies who went in to see it came back scared witless, not so much by what they saw, but by who they saw. They really caused panic amongst the people by saying that those currently inhabiting the land were 'like giants'. In short, they told the people, *'They are bigger and stronger than we are'.* (Numbers 13:31 NIV)

Their report was not the only one that came back. There was also a bold, faith-filled minority report that came back from Joshua and Caleb who saw things very differently, *'We should go up and take possession of this land, for we can certainly do it!'* (Numbers 13:30 NIV) Nonetheless, people being people, the fear of the giants held sway; faith gave in to fear and the Israelites rebelled against Moses, refusing to go into the land God had promised to give to them. Their journey had come to a juddering halt and their dream had been derailed.

After witnessing so many miracles and seeing God come through for them every day, why did the people stop trusting God? Why did they so quickly ditch their dream, the very goal they had followed since leaving Egypt when it was right in front of them? Simply, they were afraid. Giants tend to do that to us.

> *After witnessing so many miracles and seeing God come through for them every day, why did the people stop trusting God?*

The consequences of all of this were not good for the people of God at that time. For, with the exception of Caleb and Joshua, that whole generation was told by God that their disobedience and refusal to trust Him after all He had done to show them who He was, would result in them never getting to reach their goal and never entering this land. Tragically this also included the great Moses, their leader. God told Moses the awful news, *'Not one of them will ever see the land I promised on oath to their forefathers. No-one who treated me with contempt will ever see it'* (Numbers 14:23 NIV). God would keep His promise to His people, just not these people.

They had given up before they ever tried because they were so afraid of these giants that most of them had only ever heard about and had never seen with their own eyes. The story from this point until the people of God eventually enter the Promised Land in Joshua's time is laced with a deep sense of devastation as they aimlessly wander the desert for 40 years until that generation has died out and, as God promised, only Joshua and Caleb possessed what was all of theirs by right. What a waste; forty lost years, a whole generation missing their promise and all because of the fear of giants. Yes, giants are big and they are scary, but how big was their God who had shown Himself more than capable of protecting them and delivering on His word?

What is your God-given dream? What is the goal in your life that you are pursuing?

What is your God-given dream? What is the goal in your life that you are pursuing? If you got as close as they were would you just walk away when you heard of these giants? Or would you rather face your giants than face the consequence of a life lived with such deep regret? I have often thought of this as I have read this story of God's people and wonder how many of us are just at the verge of our promised land in God when we quit at the mention of the giants ahead. I was not there, so what I say now may just be bravado kicking in, but I do not think so. I think I would have been inclined to go with Joshua and Caleb and say, 'God has done it so far, why would He let us down now?'

I love the part in 'Braveheart' when in Mel Gibson's portrayal of William Wallace he stands before the Scottish troops at Stirling and speaks to this outnumbered, fearful gathering, who are voicing the fact that the enemy is bigger and stronger than they are and that to fight would mean probable death. Wallace replies, "Yes, fight and you may die, run and you will live, at least for a while. But dying in your bed many years from now, would you be willing to trade all the days from that day to this for one chance, just one chance, to come back here and tell our enemy that they may take our lives, but they will never take our freedom!"

Fear is very real, but faith is too and we have to fight one with the other. I do not think I could live with the sense of giving up on my God-given dream just because I was afraid of what I had to face to reach it. The very thought of missing my destiny would haunt me. The great American cyclist, Lance Armstrong, who overcame cancer before going on to win the Tour de France seven consecutive times, knew a lot about facing his fear and overcoming the giants that stood in his way. He was once asked what drove him on to never give up when he hit the pain-wall and when the going got tough and he gave this answer, 'Pain is temporary but quitting is forever'.

> *Fear is very real, but faith is too and we have to fight one with the other.*

Bruce Wilkinson has written an excellent book, 'The Dream Giver'[xxii] which deals with this very subject of facing our giants extensively and inventively and it is well worth reading. Wilkinson reminds his readers that whenever we reach the edge of a breakthrough for God or venture into new Kingdom territory the giants always show up. I think he is absolutely correct and this has definitely been the case in my life and ministry. I am convinced it will be the case in the lives and ministries of many of those reading this book right now. So if you are in a new place in your life and ministry which is going to require your faith in God to overcome your fear of giants, let me give you a few of the giants I have met in the past and am facing at the start of my new ministry calling in Scotland and how I believe we can overcome them.

The first giant I think we always encounter at a new juncture in our faith journey has already been mentioned, but cannot ever be ignored and it is the *giant of fear*. Fear with a capital 'F'. This is a huge giant and comes in many forms. The devil is a past master at dealing out fear to God's people. However, as much as few of us would welcome physical pain and discomfort, the fear giant we often face

xxii   Bruce Wilkinson, The Dream Giver, Multnoma Publishers Inc., 2003 on the verge of our promised land is not just confined to fear of physical danger, harm or pain. It is a much more pernicious giant than that and the sort of fear that haunts God's people hits deeper than our skin and bones. Don't ever believe the old children's rhyme, 'Sticks and stones may break your bones but names will never hurt you'. This is rubbish. I have had a few punches on the nose and belts in the mouth over the years which I have got over very quickly, but some of the criticisms from people and harsh words spoken to me have taken a lot longer to heal.

The fear giant plays on this and will taunt us with threats of failure; 'You are useless', 'You will never amount to anything' and 'You will fail at this and look stupid'. He also questions our credentials to do the job we are doing. I have had to face this a lot as I have stepped into this new calling; 'Who do you think you are?', 'What gives *you* the right to think *you* can make a difference to a nation?', 'Who do you think you are writing a book? People will think you are a bighead who thinks too much of yourself! And no-one will buy it anyway!' The fear giant usually then attacks our character threatening us with the fear of being exposed as a fraud and 'found out' for the hypocrites we truly are; 'If all those people you are speaking to now could see what you are really like!'

> *'If the opinion the world gives you of yourself makes you feel useless, get a second opinion; God's!'*

The fear giant has a loud roar and he is persistent, but he is actually more easily dealt with than one would initially think. He is disarmed when we stop listening to his opinion of us and our ministry and start listening to God's. As I once heard someone say, 'If the opinion the world gives you of yourself makes you feel useless, get a second opinion; God's!'

It is once we come to recognise who we are in Jesus and how God sees us as His sons and daughters that the fear giant's shouts and taunts are not so fearful after all. We need to remember that we have God's stamp of approval on us and we have His almighty seal of approval on our ministry. If He has called us He will equip us for that calling. Also, we must always remember that we *can, 'do all things through Christ who strengthens us'* (Philippians 4:13 NIV). The fear giant has one thing right, for what we are trying to achieve for God, we cannot actually do! But Christ in us can! If we keep our eyes fixed on Jesus and who we are in Him, we are fine and this big bully will not touch us, but if we take our eyes off Him and look to ourselves then we are in trouble. I think this is a bit like Peter walking on the water to Jesus. He was fine when he kept his eyes on the Lord, but when he looked at the water beneath him he quickly came unstuck. Alternatively it is like a child being chased by a bully, who sees his dad and runs to him; getting his dad in between himself and the bully makes all the difference.

In following this new call, the fear giant arose as I was on the edge of my new ministry and threatened me not to even bother trying to cross over into all that I knew God had for me. However, as fearful and off-putting as his shouts were, I chose to listen to the voice of God who was calling me on. So I went through all of the above and kept my eyes and ears fixed on Jesus and His word to me and I moved into my destiny. It turns out that the fear giant was not as big and fierce as he made himself out to be! I believe you will find the same too, if you walk on in faith towards your destiny, no matter how the giant of fear roars his threats at you.

The next giant I think we encounter on the edge of our breakthroughs and a new territory for God is *the money giant.* I think this giant is a hard one to shift because he has been around for a while. He is well established in the land we are trying to take and he will not roll over easily. I have known of so many good Kingdom ventures and even some that I have been involved in, which have been desperately under-funded and so many excellent ministries that are working away in our land today which are struggling as they scrape around to make ends meet. I believe that this is a disgrace to the Kingdom and it is a sure sign that the money giant has inveigled his way into the church. The money giant contests all new ministries birthed for God with the real threat that the baby will die as soon as it is born, due to the malnourishment of under-funding. The money giant's main aim is to discourage, kill faith and, in time, bury all of our Kingdom hopes and dreams.

As such it was no surprise to me that this giant arose quickly in my new ministry and continues to roar out his threats to me and to all those who are giving themselves to the work of The Scotland Trust.

The truth is that the church has always struggled with money, particularly when asked to risk investment in creative new ventures or to support ministries which think 'out of the box', even though the 'in the box' ministries are producing little or no fruit anyway. It has driven me to distraction that my own denomination has often had no problem spending millions on maintenance ministries and keeping old building open for a little while longer, while it has been slow to invest in youth work, church plants, creative arts and media and contemporary, culturally relevant outreach. This is not to mention the money we have kept in reserve for 'a rainy day'. Well, in case anyone hasn't noticed, it is pouring outside and the church is drowning. Perhaps it is time to buy some wellies and brollies and go out and reach people?

> *Everything we have is a gift from God and if we are members of His family we are accountable for how we steward it all.*

It is also a problem getting Churches, individual Christians and the Christian business community to invest in new ministries, because the money giant has convinced them of a basically flawed truth about their money and that is that it is their money! Everything we have is a gift from God and if we are members of His family we are accountable for how we steward it all. As James says; *'Every good and perfect gift comes from above, coming down from the Father'* (James 1:17 NIV); that includes money. It is not ours. It is God's and He gives it to us as a gift. Even if we think that we have got it through our own efforts and hard work, where did our energy, breath, intelligence and ability to work come from? That's right, from above!

We have all heard the adage; 'money talks'. I think this is true. Money can talk and what it says reveals what is in our hearts. It can speak from the selfishness of our heart and say, "I belong to you. You earned me and I am yours. Keep me and use me for what you want". Or it can speak from the generosity of our Spirit as God intended and say, "I can fund that mission. I can build that hospital. I can reach those young people. I can feed the hungry".

So come on people of God, open your wallets, get your cheque books out and sow some seed into the Kingdom. Whether that takes the form of being more generous to the ministry of your local church or to a compassion ministry at home or abroad or to a ministry of mission and evangelism in our land, just do something. Before I am accused of profiteering, I am not saying this particularly to ask anyone to give

So come on people of God, open your wallets, get your cheque books out and sow some seed into the Kingdom.

financial support to The Scotland Trust or my ministry. Just give to ministry! There are hundreds of them out there; good ones which are making a difference and you can help them get the job done. The only two basic Biblical principles that I suggest you follow as you do this are that you sow into good soil that is producing good fruit and that you ask the Spirit to lead you as to where you sow as He has a moment by moment up-date of where the needs are.

So whatever you do and wherever you do it, for God's sake, sow some seed into the Kingdom and together let us kill this money giant in our church and in our land for good.

If you are reading this and are struggling to make ends meet in your calling or to invest all that you need in your ministry, please be encouraged and know that despite the way it looks, God can give you the financial breakthrough you need if you keep trusting in Him and following the principles of sowing and reaping that His Word teaches. Even when the people of God are not switched on to your needs the God of His people is. A New York Pastor and friend of mine, Jack Lagatella, who knows what it means to live by faith, says this about the financial struggling that often comes with our callings, 'If it's God's will – it's God's bill!'

Finally, the third and last of what I think are the three main giants we face as we enter new ground for Jesus is *the religious giant*. I am convinced that fierce as the first two I have identified are, this is the most resistant and hardest enemy of all to faith and Kingdom progress.

Unfortunately, because the religious giant finds its home in and around the church, it contests all Kingdom progress and all moves forward into new territory for Jesus. It stands at the border and shouts, 'You cannot go there'. The religious giant also screams, 'It cannot be done this way', 'This will not work', 'We will not let you do this', 'We do not want this kind of thing or these kinds of people around here'. Please note that I am *not* personalising this by speaking about particular people in the church here, or of a way of working or a particular theological branch of the church. I am speaking of a spirit, an attitude which can affect *us all* and can appear in any place where the name and cause of Jesus is being advanced. I am convinced that the religious spirit is a direct opponent to the Spirit of God and His work. The religious spirit is a huge giant.

The religious giant hated Jesus and from the moment He made clear what He was all about it tried to kill him[xxiii]. Religion also hates all who have His Spirit, His passion and His vision, because the religious giant knows that when Jesus comes into a person's life or a community, religion dies. His freedom replaces religion's shackles and therefore, when confronted by the life and Spirit of Jesus

---

xxiii See Mark 3:6 & Luke 4:29

religion fights for its life. As I said in the previous chapter, when Jesus comes, His Kingdom displaces the kingdom of darkness and equally His Kingdom of liberation cannot co-exist with religion's rules. He came to overthrow this false god in people's lives.

There is a very interesting passage in 1 Chronicles 12:22-40 where David gathers together an army to overthrow Saul's godless kingdom and re-establish the Kingdom of God amongst His people. I believe that today God is raising an army of people around the world who are sold out to Jesus, are passionately in love with Him and are committed to seeing *His* Kingdom come and not *our* ecclesiastical or denominational empires being built.

This army is being called together by none other than the King of Kings, to overthrow the kingdom of religion which has stopped people coming to Jesus and for years has turned them away from the very place where they would have discovered His grace, healing and salvation.

So do not be surprised that when you seek to strip away all but Jesus in your life and ministry to go deeper with Him, or do new things in His name, that the religion giant will try to stop you. Religion will always contest the ground and it will fight hard. However, remember this, religion cannot kill that which is already dead! If we are dead to ourselves we are alive in Christ and the religion giant cannot kill that. Equally, religion cannot kill that which God has sent for the liberation of the captives whom He loves with an everlasting love. And even if it looks as if it has, God will simply raise it back to life again with new fervour. The religious giant thought it had killed Jesus, but He came bursting back to life with a new power and a new authority.

However, we can kill the religious giant in our life, our church and our community. Every time we die to ourselves and our agenda and live for His glory alone, we put it to death. Every time we resist the temptation to judge people, to gossip and to reject those who are not like us and instead show the grace, acceptance and love of Jesus we put a nail in the religious giant's coffin. Whenever we refuse to settle behind the walls of the churches we are in under our own man-made rules and go out with purpose to love, reach and serve those around us in Jesus' name we expose religion's lies to the world. Whenever we live the authentic Kingdom life of Jesus and those around us see His true heart revealed through us, when we take up our cross and follow Him, we defeat the religious spirit around us and people really do see the One we want them to see – Jesus.

I have identified three giants that I believe we will face as we seek to do new things and take new land for God. I know there are more and you can perhaps think of some that I have not, yet I believe that these are the three principal giants we will face on the borders of our breakthroughs. Nevertheless, the principles are the same and the same truth applies; we can bring down all of the giants that we face in our lives and ministries who contest God's call on our lives. Our God is big enough and we can do it in His name, by His word and through His Spirit. We can overthrow our giants and we can enter our promised land, whatever that is for each of us.

> *My promised land is to see a new church arise that worships Jesus with abandon and serves His world sacrificially and joyfully.*

For me it is to see a new move of God's Kingdom in Scotland that will touch the broken, heal the sick, save the lost and totally transform the church. My promised land is to see a new church arise that worships Jesus with abandon and serves His world sacrificially and joyfully; a church with confidence in itself and its calling, because its confidence is in its Lord.

In these days, these historic days of entering new places and standing on the verge of new things for God, I pray that many will arise in our nation and around the world who will not listen to the majority report that says our enemy is bigger and stronger than us, but will have the Caleb spirit that says, 'We should go up and take possession of this land, for we can certainly do it!' We certainly can!

CHAPTER 13: NORTHERN LIGHTS

'Arise, shine, for your light has come and the glory of the Lord rises upon you'

ISAIAH 60:1-3 NIV

Most Scots will know the song, *'The Northern Lights of old Aberdeen'*, which speaks of the 'Aurora Borealis', a spectacular natural phenomenon where patterns of light appear on a clear, dark night to illuminate the sky. This can occasionally be seen in the night sky over Britain, particularly in the north and has been synonymous with the city of Aberdeen. I have lived in Aberdeen for eight years, but have only seen the 'northern lights' properly on one occasion. Once seen, though, this sight is never forgotten. It lights up the sky in a wonderful and unique way and the light display on show gives the impression, as the song says, of 'heavenly dancers in the sky'.

Isaiah speaks of a spiritual 'Aurora Borealis' that will arise over the people of God and will cause such light to shine from them that it cannot be missed. This light will be the glory of God and it will be a global phenomenon that will cause thick darkness to be dispersed and people from all nations to come to it; magnetically drawn like a moth is to a porch light. Isaiah says, *'Arise, shine, for your light has come and the glory of the Lord rises upon you. See, darkness covers the earth and thick darkness is over the peoples, but the glory of the Lord rises over you. Nations will come to your light and kings to the brightness of your dawn.'* (Isaiah 60:1-3 NIV)

> How I long for such a day to arise over the earth and particularly in our land of Scotland. I believe it is closer than ever.

How I long for such a day to arise over the earth and particularly in our land of Scotland. I believe it is closer than ever. The darkness always seems dark, yet for these last few generations, the darkness has seemed somehow darker. Isaiah encourages us that the thicker the darkness, the more imminent the coming of the light; as the proverb says, "It's always darkest before the dawn."

The Christian church has always seen itself as a community of light amidst the world's darkness. There are numerous references to this in Jesus' ministry and the New Testament Epistles and I particularly like what Paul says in Ephesians 5:8 about what it means to be a follower of Jesus, *"For you were once darkness, but now you are light in the Lord. Live as children of light"*. These are not metaphors but ontological statements of fact; 'You *were* darkness' and 'You *are* light'. If we could just grasp the full significance of this how much more effective and confident we would be in our mission as we daily lived as glowing Jesus-lights in the world around us – a bit like the 'Ready Brek' kid in the old adverts!

I would love to challenge the church in Scotland to see ourselves as God sees us; children of light who have all that we need already within us to penetrate the darkness around us and see the Kingdom light shine here, in our day. Furthermore, to realise that if we are children of light who live in the northern part of

> *I would love to challenge the church in Scotland to see ourselves as God sees us*

the northern hemisphere we are 'northern lights' who can become such a spectacular display of God's splendour and glory that our spiritual 'Aurora Borealis' draws many to Jesus, in this nation and from the nations of the earth.

To do this we need to really start believing in ourselves and all we have to give. As a nation we Scots can be very self-effacing and in the church in Scotland this can be even worse. My friend Peter Neilson and I were discussing this once and, as always, he had a stunning insight to hand! He told me of a book he had just read which was written by an author with a Scots' background living in America. He said the author argued that at a deep level Scots and Americans were very similar in their basic understanding that we are all equal; as Scots put it, *'We're all Jock Tamson's bairns'*. However, the difference in how this works itself out in practice, gives a stunning insight into where we differ. Peter said that the author concluded that this inherent truth of equality for the Americans meant that 'everyone was special', but for Scots it meant 'no-one was special'. So we can grow up with this lie that we should not try to be anything special and never try to 'get ideas above our station' and I believe that this has deterred us from appreciating and pursuing our own gifts and abilities, particularly in the church.

I have read and heard Jack Deere [xxiv] speak on the prophetic heritage of Scotland. His writing and teaching is brilliant and inspirational, but as I read and then listened to him share, I was deeply frustrated by it all. I was not frustrated by Jack, far from it; I honour him for feeding my soul and the church in Scotland so well. My frustration was with my contemporaries and with myself. Had we gone so far back that we needed someone from America to remind us and teach us of the prophetic heritage of our own country and wake us up to who we are and all we could be in Christ? What had we been doing?

I have lost count of the number of times when an event or meeting is only deemed worth going to if there is a 'big-name' speaker or band from down south, America, Australia etc. In the past, I have been as guilty of seeing things in this way as anyone else. It is almost as if the 'stars' of the Christian world coming to Scotland will be able to shine some light into our otherwise dim spiritual world. It's great that these folks have a heart for us and are prepared to come and share their ministry and I am not saying we should be parochial and never have visitors or travelling ministries, that is not my point at all. I just feel that we should not have to depend so much on importing speakers, worship leaders, bands and ministries but that instead, we should start raising our own up.

---

xxiv Jack Deere, *Surprised by the Power of The Spirit*, Zondervan, 1996

It may seem a strange analogy at first, but look at how quickly football in Scotland stopped producing great young players when the market was flooded with foreign imports. Only when it became apparent that this was not good for the game long-term, did the clubs start investing in local development. English football is now recognising this problem too at the highest level of their sport.

I also get very frustrated when I go into a Christian bookstore in a Scottish town or city and see the dearth of books, CDs and resources by Scottish authors, writers or artists. The last time I looked in one well known Christian bookstore franchise there were no Scottish authors in the best-selling list and after looking through over 80 newly produced CDs searching for a Scottish singer, worship leader or band I had found none. It's not as if we have no talent and creativity in us; just think about the amount of inventions which are now in daily use that have a Scottish origin.

It is time for the church in Scotland to trust in ourselves and the gifts and talents God has placed in His people here and both rejoice in them and release them. If there is someone in your church who has a passion to preach or pastor; to be an evangelist or teacher; to lead worship or reach out to the poor, then encourage them to do it and help them to find opportunities to express these gifts. This is particularly true with the younger generation. Let's not make them pew-fillers for twenty years before they get a chance to exercise their ministry, or leave before they get that far. Let's invest in them, mentor them, train them and release them to minister now.

> *It is time for the church in Scotland to trust in ourselves and the gifts and talents God has placed in His people here and both rejoice in them and release them.*

I long for the time when we get together in our thousands not because of a 'big name' ministry, but because we have come to worship a big God who has a big heart for the people of our nation. I have a dream, which The Scotland Trust leaders all share, to gather the church in our land together for such a time to worship and pray at Murrayfield or Hampden and for us to cry out to God for our own nation. As I have said earlier, we need to take responsibility for reaching the people of our own nation. The bonus is that when we do, they understand us and we understand them. No-one knows the uniqueness of a culture better than a native of that place. Since I began speaking at engagements in my role with The Scotland Trust, I have been greatly encouraged by the response of people around the country who have heard me and said how good it was to hear someone speak with such passion and feeling for their own nation. One man in Orkney added, 'It's great to hear that sort of preaching with a Scottish accent'.

To my delight, when I tell people I am writing a book, I have always been met with encouragement and anticipation for what I have to share, rather than the negative responses I stereotypically and mistakenly expected I would get from my compatriots. I have been thrilled that at least a dozen people to whom I have spoken, have said it has encouraged them to write too as they have something they feel is worth sharing.

The thinking may be, *'Well if Jim can write a book anyone can!'* Nonetheless, that is fine by me as long as people are using their gifts. I think most people have a book in them and we all have something unique that only we can share with the world. There may also be singers, dancers, artists and a host of other talented people reading this book who have never felt they were good enough to share their gift with the church and the world. Can I encourage you to go for it! You will never know until you try. As a Christian songwriter in my 40s it is another dream of mine to see young song-writers come to the fore in churches all across the land, sharing their songs and leading God's people in them in their own locality. Long-term I would love to create a centre of training in excellence in Scotland for Christian

Can I encourage you to go for it! You will never know until you try.

artists a bit like the one Ray and Nancy Goudie have developed in Bristol called *New Generation Music and Mission.*

Another area we Scottish Christians have to confront, is our apparent lack of passion, or our fear of expressing it in worship and ministry, particularly amongst men. We can show a very dour and reserved exterior which we claim is cultural, but I am not so sure. I have often challenged men in church, a lot of whom are my friends, that they will sing, shout and dance at football or rugby matches, ceilidhs and nights out at the pub, but become highly-reserved, emotionless guys when it comes to worship and the things of God. Is it any wonder the world thinks we are boring?

I do not accept this and feel it undersells the church and the Lord and again I say this because I have been there. It perpetuates the myth that church is a woman's activity and gives very few real role models to young guys in the church. So I have often challenged my mates to begin by giving as least as much to worship and service as they do to football, or whatever their leisure outlet is and see how it transforms their Christian life. I am not advocating plastic Christianity which is all froth and no substance, but to see real, deep, joyful and passionate people (including men) following Jesus today in our land, would indeed

> *I have often challenged my mates to begin by giving as least as much to worship and service as they do to football.*

switch some lights on for the world that sits in darkness looking for something to believe in.

Finally, as a church in this nation in this time we must keep following our heart, dreaming our dreams and continuing to have vision. If we do not, what is the alternative? We die; *'Where there is no vision, the people perish'* (Proverbs 29:18 KJV). I was recently driving up to Ullapool and as I did I passed some of the most beautiful mountains and glens, lochs and valleys there are. As I passed one particular glen, seated at the foot of the hills was a herd of deer. These were not the small red deer I have seen many times driving through the lowlands, these were the guys who appear on postcards and bottles of whisky! They were the authentic 'Monarchs of the Glen' and they were in every way majestic. I stopped for a few minutes to watch them and was thrilled to watch these magnificent creatures in their own environment behaving perfectly naturally; free to run as they pleased.

On the way back down the road to Inverness, I was about to pass the same spot and wondered if I would see them again. To my great sadness I only saw one and he was lying dead at the side of the road, obviously having been struck down by a car or truck. It was a pathetic sight to see this deer lying dead, just a few days after I had seen so many, and perhaps even this one, alive and free. It reminded me that we only have an allotted time to live our dreams and be all we can be before it is too late because, like this deer, we never know what is around the corner. But at least before he died this deer was living the life he was meant to live. The same cannot be said of all the people I have met in my life and many of them are in church; people who have never felt the exhilaration of chasing their dream and living the life they were born to live.

I have heard it said that the two most important dates in your life are the day you are born and the day you discover why! As God does a new thing around the world and in our land I believe that more and more people will start to discover that second destiny date; the day they know why they were born, the reason for which they were put on this earth. As they do and then walk purposefully into that destiny with confidence, I am convinced that the 'new wineskin' church that is emerging will start to take real shape and become very visible indeed.

What were you born for? Who were you born to be? If you have not discovered that yet, then ask God to show you.

I particularly pray this for Scotland.

What were you born for? Who were you born to be? If you have not discovered that yet, then ask God to show you and do not let go of Him until you know what it is. I believe that God has placed a multitude of dreams and visions in His people in Scotland and I want to encourage you to unearth them, pursue them and never stop until you are living them.

Our nation needs your vision to come to pass and your dream to be revealed. So does your church, community, city, friends and family. God gave it to you to bless them! So whatever it is, go for it. I am going for mine and while it is never easy, sometimes scary, often difficult and always hard work, it is also exhilarating and the only way to live. What's more I happen to believe that without me living it the world is a darker place. I know the same is true for what God has put in you.

We are the people of God in this land. We are the 'northern lights' He has called to this time and this place and it is for us and us alone to *'shine like stars in the universe as (we) hold out the word of life'* (Philippians 2:15 NIV) to Scotland.

CHAPTER 14: REACHING FOR MORE!

'We're reaching for more; we're hungry for more of You. We're desperate that You come and make us to be like You. So won't You come, won't You come Lord Jesus'

The most amazing part about becoming a Christian is the discovery that God loves us and accepts us just as we are. When we first respond to Him in faith it does not matter who we are, where we have been and what we have done; we come as we are, warts and all and He welcomes us into His family on those terms – absolutely no pre-conditions! For any new believer this discovery is an awesome and humbling one.

Yet as our relationship with Him deepens and grows it becomes equally clear that He is not finished with us. He is working in us and with us to change us. Not because He did not particularly like us when He first got to know us. Nothing could be further from the truth! God asked His precious Son Jesus to lay down His life for us in the full knowledge of *just* how sinful and rotten we were and would be at our very worst. God's unconditional and gracious love is not in question. The reason God keeps working on us from the moment of our new birth in Christ until the day we stand complete before Him at the end of our lives is because He wants to make something incredible out of us. He wants us to become like Jesus.

> *The most amazing part about becoming a Christian is the discovery that God loves us and accepts us just as we are.*

I have five wonderful children and when each of them was born I was there at their birth giving Maggie all the love and support I could; I know there was not much else I could do! I loved watching my children being born. By the time Gavin, our fifth child, entered the world, we were a bit more used to this moment than we were when our first, Pam, appeared thirteen years earlier, yet it was just as special as that very first time. Each new birth was wonderful and each new life something amazing to behold. My favourite moment was always a few minutes after each child was born when I got to hold them and sit with them for the first time. Looking into this little face for the first time, deeply in awe at God's creation and madly in love with this tiny bundle of fragile life that I had just been introduced to, is one of the most magical moments life has brought my way.

However, magical as this first moment is and spell-binding as each newborn child was to me right then, as their father, I would never want them to stay that way for good. As incredible as they were then, something very wrong would have been happening if years later they were still in that vulnerable and fragile state. It is exactly the same with our spiritual birth. It is a unique new experience and a moment not to be forgotten, but we are not meant to stay there for good and it's the last thing our heavenly Father wants. God wants us to grow. We were born to grow; we need to grow and the church and the world need us to grow if we are to fulfil the destiny God has for us and touch the world in our own special way.

> *God wants us to grow. We were born to grow; we need to grow and the church and the world need us to grow.*

If we, as individual Christians need to continually grow into the mature followers of Jesus that God wants us to be, then it is equally the case that the corporate body of Christ has to grow too. God wants mature churches and communities of faith that are striving to be all they can be in Him. In fact more than just wanting this, I am convinced God *expects* this!

I think the secret to growth, both personal and corporate is never to be content with where we are and to be always reaching for more. Very early on in my walk with Jesus and as I served Him, I developed what I would call a Godly-discontent. This was not the sort of discontent one would associate with ingratitude or spoiled immaturity, but a discontent that was rooted in an understanding of how huge God is and how much more of Him we need to know and subsequently how much more we can become in Him. This is an attitude which marks those in any walk in life who long to make a bigger difference; who want to cast a bigger shadow. I want to be one of them and I would encourage you to be one of them too!

I used to have a theory that some people in life had a 'success gene', something that made them better at what they did than others, whether that was in sport, art, music, business or any other field. This may or may not be true, but what I am convinced is true is that there are some people who have an 'success attitude', or as I heard one of my American friends over in Aberdeen working in the oil industry call it, 'the can-do attitude'. Maggie and I also have some great friends in Canada, Charlie and Sue Kopczyk, who have a fantastic ministry to the poor, homeless and those trapped in crime and addiction in their city called, 'Why not?' Their attitude is summed up in their mission statement, *'Some people see things and ask why? We dream things and say... why not!'* Christians are meant to be 'over-comers', we were made to make a difference and the bigger the better.

We hear a lot these days about the carbon footprint we all leave on this planet. Similarly, in forensic investigation we are told that everyone leaves a genetic fingerprint behind them wherever they go. Well, I am also convinced that we all leave something far more permanent as a legacy on this earth, our soul imprint. I often ask myself, 'What soul imprint will I leave on this earth?' What imprint do you, your church and your ministry leave on the heart and soul of your community? I want to encourage you to be people who always reach for more in your life, knowing that the more we reach for, the bigger the imprint we will make.

> *I am also convinced that we all leave something far more permanent as a legacy on this earth, our soul imprint.*

In the last two years of my ministry at Oldmachar we emphasised 'reaching for more' as our goal and it was, for me, the overall theme and in all that we did; as we did it with a heart that wanted more. I even had my friend, Andi Tooth, who runs a printing and graphics business in Glasgow make me two huge graphic art displays of two arms reaching high to God in worship with the words 'reaching for more' written under them. These were hung at either side of the front of the church above the main platform. They are powerful images and I wanted them to be a visual statement of intent for all who came to worship in the church.

I also wrote a worship song of the same title which I taught the congregation and we often sang this with our own hearts and hands lifted high. The chorus says, "We're reaching for more; we're hungry for more of You. We're desperate that You come and make us to be like You. So won't You come; won't You come Lord Jesus". He always did! In closing this book there are a few things I would like to encourage you to reach for more of in your life and ministry, both as an individual disciple of Jesus and as the community of disciples we call the church.

Reach for more in worship. It is not possible to obey the Greatest Commandment to love God with all our heart, soul, mind and strength[xxv] without reaching for more in worship. It is also the key to ushering in the very presence of God;[xxvi] and when God comes He changes everything. So if you want your church to become more, worship more!

Reach for more love. This flows from the first commandment into how we manage to live the second, to 'Love your neighbour as yourself' (Matthew 22:38 NIV). The more we love God, the more we love each other and the more we love the world. Our passion for God drives our compassion for His children. The one place where

---

xxv See Matthew 22:37
xxvi See John 4:23-24

people should feel a different level of love is in the community of faith that follows Jesus. Love draws people and it makes them stay.

Reach for more in prayer. Prayer changes things. This may be a cliché, but it is true nonetheless. The greatest breakthroughs in our lives and ministries come when we reach for more in our prayer life. A season of fifty days of prayer in Oldmachar changed the church. It came as a combination of people just wanting to be in God's presence more when we did pray and also expecting to see more happen as a result of our prayers. This looks very much like the way Jesus' prayer ministry worked. Being in the secret place with His Father empowered His public ministry and He never seemed to doubt that the Father would hear and answer Him.

> *Reach for more in God's Word. This is where we feed our souls and receive our revelation.*

Reach for more in God's Word. This is where we feed our souls and receive our revelation. Without it we become weak and uncertain in our faith; with it there is an immoveable anchor to hold us in the fiercest storms. I have also begun to read God's Word much less as a narrative and write myself, my family and my ministry into its story and to trust the promises of God in every area of my life. I believe this is what it means to take God at His Word.

Reach for more grace. A community of faith that is not a community of grace is a disgrace! Let's be honest, we all know times when the church has been like that. We do not have to think too hard to recall times when we, or others around us, have operated without grace and it has a deadly effect on the church.

We can take God's grace so freely then give it so sparingly. I believe that the single most effective 'tool' in the ministry at Oldmachar that brought people to Jesus and kept them with Him and us was the atmosphere of grace under which we learned to live.

Reach for more people. The Parable of the Sower, in Luke 8:5-8, is a stunning arithmetical wake up call for the church's evangelism. In it, Jesus says that of every four seeds we sow only one will make it to full growth. So if we want to reach people for Jesus we need to sow a lot of seeds! If you only have one person in your life whom you are influencing with the Gospel, you need more friends! If your church is only touching five percent of your community in its outreach, do not brace yourself for a major explosion of new people any time soon. However, if we sow seed abundantly we should prepare for, even expect more people. I can never understand some church leaders who almost see growth as a bad thing. I know that big is not always beautiful, but neither is small. I have been around both and I know which one I prefer. This does not have to be the day of small things; there is a huge harvest ahead for all who will sow liberally.

Reach for more relevance. As a church we should refuse to be irrelevant. Jesus was the master communicator and He was always culturally relevant. Our communication skills and strategies are extremely important for us to get right. We compete with a world which does communication with a billion dollar budget, so

> *Reach for more relevance. As a church we should refuse to be irrelevant.*

our photocopied leaflets knocked up on a home p.c. will not attract people just because we stick them through their letter box. We should strive for excellence in all we do, as we hold out to the world in a relevant way, the hope that we have. Those whom we want to come and listen to our sermons, or engage with our worship music on Sundays, particularly those under forty, are used to watching 'Peter Kay live' DVDs and T in the Park gigs. This should at least give us something to think about as we prepare our public worship. To be more relevant does not mean we need to dilute our content but make it creative and engaging, otherwise all the amazing truths we hope to communicate can get lost to our modern listeners.

Reach for more insight. In the passage from 1 Chronicles 12 which I refer to in chapter 12 there is mention of 'the sons of Issachar', whom the text explains, *'understood the times and knew what Israel should do'* (1 Chronicles 12:32 NIV). This says two things to me; firstly that they had an insight into the culture in which they lived and secondly that they had an insight into the heart and mind of God for that time. These were the men who would give the army its insight and strategy for the fight ahead. I pray that many sons and daughters of Issachar will arise in the midst of God's army in Scotland in this generation; and I pray for the church in Scotland today that we will understand that *this is our time* and that we will know what God is calling us to do for such a time as this.

ABOUT THE SCOTLAND TRUST

What is the Vision of The Scotland Trust?

At the heart of The Scotland Trust is a desire to see revival in our nation and to encourage churches in our land to become all that God has destined them to be!

Our core belief is that not only can we see this happen but we can dare to believe that it is imminent and that we are the generation who are going to see it and live in it.

The vision is to encourage a grassroots movement in Scotland that will bring about radical spiritual and social transformation of this nation.

What will The Scotland Trust do?

Our main aim is to: Raise up the people of Scotland to believe in their gifts and calling and to use them to reach our nation today. How this will happen is by;

1. **Community Transformation:**
   Planting creative music and sports mission teams across the nation in partnership with local churches and other ministries

2. **Training:**
   Creating a Training Centre of Excellence to equip people who are called to reach this nation in new and creative ways

3. **Culturally Relevant Outreach:**
   Offering mission resources and consultancy for churches and ministries across the country

4. **Inspiring the Church:**
   Bringing the church in the nation together for days of worship and prayer for our nation

5. **Equipping the church:**
   Providing resources; books, CD's, worship albums – all birthed in the Scottish Church with Scotland's new sound and fragrance.

CONTACT DETAILS

If you wish to contact Jim Ritchie, hear more about The Scotland Trust or become a prayer or financial partner of this exciting new ministry please contact Jim at:

The Scotland Trust
68 Hammerman Drive
Aberdeen, AB24 4SH
Tel: 01224 484332
Email – enquiries@scotland-trust.org.uk
www.scotland-trust.org.uk